THE

KETO

THERAPY

Over 180 AIP, Paleo, Dairy-Free, Non-Gluten, Whole and Grain-less Allergy-Friendly Ketogenic recipes for healing and weight loss

By

Jessica Smith

INTRODUCTION

Doubling up on Keto and Healthy feeding can be a fantastic way to improve your immune system, promote gut health and lose weight while watching your allergies

There are a lot of people following a keto diet who, to my way of thinking, still consume processed foods and sweeteners which don't raise blood glucose but which could lead to an autoimmune flare. These same individuals may also consume sugar in foods which have low overall carbs.

Cutting out potentially harmful content like Gluten, Dairy, soy while emphasizing on weight loss seems impossible especially since most of the ketogenic recipes are diary related.

After 18 years of fighting multiple autoimmune diseases with traditional western meds, I was to a point where the meds no longer helped. My doctor said there was nothing that could help.

I researched and found different diets that could help majorly the Autoimmune Paleo Diet Protocol and the Paleo Diet itself. Within a month I was off all meds and felt better than in years. (This was 2 years ago.) I've stayed with it but have flares as illness or anxiety/worry get the better of me.

I come from a family with strong ancestral allergy, I have a multiple autoimmune diseases, my mum is highly gluten sensitive, Lactose/Dairy protein intolerant and diabetic. And this has led to so many health issues that pushed us to transit from one diet to another including Whole30, Veganism, Paleo but its either the diet takes care of my health issue without significantly reducing weight or vice versa

Generally, The Keto Therapy focuses on the use of whole, paleo, nutrient-dense and clean foods for healing purposes while unhealthy processed and packaged food will be seriously eliminated in this diet. This helps to:

- Provide abundant energy
- Reduce inflammation
- Increase mental clarity

- Reduce the risk of chronic diseases like type ii diabetes and heart disease
- Possibly prevent and even reverse early alzheimer's
- Promote weight loss
- Reduce abdominal cramps
- Reduce bloating and diarrhea
- Minimizing, stomach or intestinal pain and gassiness (burping or flatulence)
- Indigestion and **many others**

The book contains over 180 recipes with nutritional information for all 7 basic allergies and diet which include but not limited to AIP, Paleo, Gluten Free, Paleo, Grain Free, Nut Free, Sugar Free, Soy Free and Whole.

The mouthwatering recipes are classified in Breakfast, Main Dishes and Side Dishes, very easy to make and will help you lose weight while nourishing your body.

THE KETOGENIC DIET

A Quick Review of Fats

Fat is an important macronutrient that has unfortunately been vilified for decades. Emerging research shows that all of the low-fat advice we grew up with was unfounded and fat doesn't lead to obesity and heart disease.

THE ROLE OF FAT IN THE BODY:

- Helps form our cell membranes
- Offers us a rich source of energy
- Protects our nervous system
- Helps us make hormones
- Forms our brains
- Supports effective functioning of the nervous system
- Nourishes our skin from the inside out
- Stabilizes blood sugar levels
- Lubricates our joints

All crucial stuff, right? So you can see why eliminating it could potentially cause us harm, while eating more of it can benefit our health and wellness.

What is a Ketogenic Diet?

The ketogenic diet, which is a high fat and very low carb diet, has recently become a popular choice for people wanting to lose weight and a few inches.

Historically, the diet has been used to help with the symptoms of pediatric epilepsy, until pharmaceutical companies took over with antiepileptic agents.

The ketogenic diet puts our body in a state of ketosis — where it burns fat, either from food or within our own fat cells, for fuel. Fat becomes the main source for fuel, as opposed to glucose from carbohydrates and sugar.

Low-carbohydrate diets, such as the ketogenic diet, have been used as ways to reduce body fat. Part of this weight loss is due to caloric restriction, as a result of the removal of a significant amount of carbohydrates. Traditional ketogenic diets generally limit the intake of carbohydrates from fruit, grains, and starches to fewer than 15 grams per day; however, different people have different thresholds of how many carbohydrates they can consume without being "kicked out" of the state of ketosis.

Those following a ketogenic diet consume liberal amounts of fat, moderate protein, and non-starchy vegetables, and focus less on consuming foods that contain higher amounts of carbohydrates. This makes the diet very satiating, and for the most part, easier to follow than other diets due to the abundance of fats that help to satisfy us.

There are benefits of a ketogenic diet which I'll dive into further as you read along, but in short, it can help to improve energy, blood sugar balance, pain, inflammation, migraines, and oxidative stress. It may also contribute to better brain function and mood regulation. Research has shown that ketogenic diets may be helpful in a variety of conditions, ranging from neurological issues, including multiple sclerosis and epilepsy, to reactive hypoglycemia. However, there are some precautions to consider.

How Does a Ketogenic Diet Work?

To understand how ketogenic diets work, we first need to take a look at how the body converts the food it takes in, to the fuel that powers our cells.

The body typically utilizes glucose as its primary fuel source. When it doesn't receive glucose from dietary sources, the body looks to its energy storage units, called glycogen. Muscle cells contain glycogen, but most of the glycogen our body utilizes comes from the liver. However, the liver can only store about 100 grams (or 400 calories) of glycogen, which can quickly become depleted.

When we no longer have sufficient levels of glucose (either from food, or from glycogen, the body's backup glucose), the body doesn't just shut down. Instead, we have a backup fuel called ketone bodies, or ketones.

Ketones are water-soluble molecules, produced in the liver from fatty acids. There are three types of ketones – β-hydroxybutyrate (BHB), acetoacetate, and acetone. These ketones can become the brain and body's main energy source when glucose is not available.

Restricting one's carbohydrate intake can shift the body's fuel source from glucose to ketones, as this limits circulating blood sugars. This shifts the body from utilizing glucose to utilizing fat, which gets repackaged as ketones. This metabolic state, in which some of the body's energy supply comes from ketone bodies in the blood, is called ketosis. Fasting or starvation can put the body's metabolism into a state of ketosis, as can a very low-carbohydrate, high-fat ketogenic diet.

What Does a Ketogenic Diet Look Like?

The classic ketogenic diet contains a 4:1 ratio by weight of fat to combined protein and carbohydrates. Ketosis typically occurs within two to four days of eating fewer than 20-50 grams of carbohydrates daily, although everyone has a different metabolism, and individual results will vary.

While this amount of fat is far more than what most people eat in their diet, it may not necessarily be unhealthy. Although dietary fat once got a bad reputation, today we see that fat quality is a more important factor, and that certain fats, like coconut milk and avocados, can even have health benefits. (You can read more about the benefits of good fats here.)

In the traditional ketogenic diet, high-fat foods, including various meats, eggs, cheese, fish, nuts and seeds, avocado, butter, and oils, form the foundation. A few other foods, such as non-starchy vegetables and small amounts of berries, lemons, and limes, are also allowed. Keep reading to see how to tailor a ketogenic diet to compliment a Hashimoto's healing journey.

INTRODUCTION TO KETOGENIC AUTOIMMUNE PROTOCOL DIET

What Are Allergies?

I know we all have experienced an allergy attack at some point, even just once, but do you know what allergies are and why they come?

Let's have a look to better understand the mechanism of allergies and how to avoid them.

First of all, allergies are a reaction of the immune system to a foreign substance which has entered the body. All kind of substances enter the body at all times (including foods) so what is that can trigger an allergy reaction at times?

There are 5 root causes of an immune response:

- a genetic cause (like your blood type)
- a cause of toxicity (Chemical toxins, heavy metals, irritants etc.)
- a nutritional deficiency (lack of vitamins or minerals)
- an infectious cause (presence of bacteria)
- an emotional cause (high stress or a traumatic event)

Now the immune response (allergy) is only one of the ways these underlying causes can manifest themselves in the body. Inflammation, thyroid and adrenal malfunction and depression are some examples of other ways the body can react.

What to Do to Eliminate Allergies?

1. The main focus is of course to identify and eliminate the underlying cause or causes. To assess what the cause is a variety of tests can be performed, depending on the type of allergy and what part of the body they affect.
2. An example of tests can be IgE-based skin tests, IcG blood tests, electro dermal test, pulse test etc.
3. Finding the root cause is of vital importance and it is what separates Foundational Nutrition from any other kind of nutrition and the medical establishment. Foundational Nutrition investigates the underlying causes of disease and seeks to address them.
4. If you give a supplement to relieve the symptoms of an allergy it is better than giving a medication, but the approach is the same. You need a different approach to solve the real cause which creates the problem!
5. Once the cause is determined a plan of action can be made. Most of the times the number one focus is digestion.

Digestion and Its Role in Allergies.

Why is digestion so important in controlling and preventing allergies?

- Our digestive system is the main entryway for allergens
- It is the largest immune organ in the body
- Contains the largest number of neurotransmitters
- We absorb nutrients through it
- It is an organ of detoxification.

For example, if the intestinal mucosa is compromised, by inflammation, autoimmunity or symptoms of IBS, Macronutrients will able to penetrate into the blood stream, where they are not recognized as nutrients at all, but they are attacked as enemies to the body, creating antigens.

A large quantity of antigens leads to higher inflammation and autoimmune conditions. This is a vicious cycle that can only be corrected by repairing the leaky gut therefore getting rid of the root cause.

The Role OF Diet

- In order to repair our digestive system diet is paramount.
- Removing the offending foods is the pre-requisite for healing to take place.
- The foods that most commonly seem to be implicated in creating antigens are: cereals (wheat, spelt, millet etc.) dairy products, caffeine, yeast and citrus fruits.
- A Therapeutic Ketogenic Diet addresses the issue of allergens in the diet, eliminating most offending foods, giving the body the necessary conditions for healing.
- When combined with the principles of Foundational Nutrition, a Therapeutic Ketogenic Diet can be most effective in finding the root causes, providing adequate nutritional support and avoiding offending foods, creating the best possible scenario for healing.
- That means not just masking a symptom, but truly healing the body's systems so they can again function the way they were designed.

Why Ketogenic AIP?

Why would I restrict even more and begin a ketogenic AIP diet??

THERE IS STRONG SCIENTIFIC EVIDENCE THAT A KETOGENIC DIET CAN:

- provide abundant energy
- reduce inflammation
- increase mental clarity
- reduce the risk of chronic diseases like type II diabetes and heart disease
- possibly prevent and even reverse early Alzheimer's
- promote weight loss

WHAT IS A STRICT KETOGENIC DIET, ANYWAY?

- 20 g or less of total carbs a day
- moderate to high protein depending on your needs
- high amounts of healthy fat (e.g. lard, tallow, olive oil, coconut oil, butter)

There are a lot of people following a keto diet who, to my way of thinking, still consume processed foods and sweeteners which don't raise blood glucose but which could lead to an autoimmune flare. These same individuals may also consume sugar in foods which have low overall carbs.

Food to Avoid for Ketogenic AIP

If you want to combine AIP and Keto and begin a ketogenic AIP diet you will still need to avoid the following unless you have reintroduced them:

- Nuts and seeds
- Nightshades (e.g. potatoes, tomatoes, peppers, spices from peppers)
- Processed foods
- dairy
- eggs

LIMIT CARBS:

- On top of that you will need to limit carbs:
- no starchy tubers or below ground vegetables (no yams ... sob)
- moderate onion consumption
- Little sugar, honey, maple syrup or other high carb sweeteners

AVOID THE FOLLOWING FOR LIFE IF YOU HAVE AN AUTOIMMUNE
DISEASE:

- Unhealthy fats: cottonseed oil (think Crisco), safflower oil, soybean oil,
  corn oil, and canola oil)
- Gluten
- Beans and legumes
- Grains and grain-like seeds

It sounds like this Ketogenic AIP is even more restrictive than AIP and, in some
respects it is, but I found it MUCH MUCH easier to incorporate this into my life
as compared to AIP which I found VERY VERY hard at the beginning.

Maybe I am just used to eating in a restricted fashion but I didn't find it nearly as
hard to start Ketogenic AIP.

The biggest time consumer at the BEGINNING of this diet can be tracking carbs,
fats, and proteins (these are called macros). You can get a very inexpensive online
calculator called Cron-o-meter or get it for free if you don't mind the odd ad.

This one will calculate both macronutrients and micro-nutrients and you can set
it for the ketogenic macros that you are aiming for.

However, we all want to make things easier on ourselves so once you have a
handle on what 20 g or less of carbs looks like (it is not much) then you won't
need to calculate macros anymore.

In a typical day, I would eat maybe a cup of broccoli, a green salad with oil and
vinegar dressing, 1/4 cup of blueberries with 1/3 cup homemade coconut yogurt
plus fatty meat or fish at each meal.

What you stand to gain on Ketogenic AIP

1. Funnily enough, reduced anxiety (I have never thought of myself as an
   anxious person but I have a new level of calm)
2. Anti-aging benefit and risk of chronic disease reduction (hopefully
   happening as we speak)
3. Skin tag which can be a sign of insulin resistance dried up and fell off

Are you curious about the keto diet? It seems to be taking over, growing rapidly
in popularity, and spreading faster than the paleo movement ever did. How
different are they? Is it KETO VS PALEO? Are these two lifestyles competing or
can they work together in harmony?

As a lifelong foodie, chef and self-made healing diet expert, I am going to break
down the difference between paleo and keto. Explain the benefits to both and
even explain the benefits of the autoimmune protocol, and why an elimination
diet could be exactly what you need to really kick start your healing journey.

Whether you're looking at paleo or keto for weight loss, to reduce inflammation or reverse chronic disease the foundation for success with any lifestyle change is information!

LET'S BREAK IT DOWN

Autoimmune Protocol (AIP) is an elimination diet which removes any and all possible inflammatory foods from your diet. The foods removed all contain higher levels of anti-nutrients, which are essentially the plants defense mechanism. Everything in nature has it.

These foods, which were once alive, contain substances that make them hard to digest or otherwise unattractive as a food source to possible threats. When a person with leaky gut ingests these foods, they can permeate the gut and these inflammatory substances will then get a ride on the lymphatic system or blood stream.

This causes the immune system to attack healthy cells and cause inflammation. For folks with arthritis- in the joints, for folks with my condition Hidradenitis Suppurativa it's in hair follicles, for Hashimoto's it's the thyroid and so on.

So yes, leaky gut, is exactly that, leaky, as in these anti-nutrients escape the digestive track and go cause problems in your body, usually in the form of inflammation.

The foods to avoid are vast, and I will say MOST people do not react to all of these foods, but the point is that you remove all possible trigger foods from your diet until you see improvement, then you add these foods in one at a time. Observe. Take notes. Go slow... and the culprits will show their face.

Last year the first medical study for the efficacy of the AIP was performed. The participants all had Ulcerative Colitis. The results were amazing with about 70% of the subjects improving or finding remission.

The Difference between AIP, Paleo and Keto AIP:

AUTOIMMUNE PROTOCOL

AIP is not a low carb diet, although some folks have found that doing a keto/AIP is very useful. However, it can be VERY restricting, starches are a main source of calories in AIP and used for all sorts of baking and binding.

The AIP is NOT meant to be a forever diet. This ELIMINATION DIET is a tool. Once you learn your trigger foods, you should be able to enjoy a variety of foods that do not make you flare. Most folks stay paleo or go keto after this.

PALEO

The paleo diet is widely known as the caveman diet, but it has greatly evolved from just trying to mimic the eating habits of prehistoric man (and woman). The basis of paleo is to avoid all grains, gluten and processed foods.

Think foods that you could eat without farming. Foods that you could forage, animals you could hunt. Yet, we live in a modern time, where we make flour from coconuts! So while cavemen certainly didn't have access to ghee or almond meal, these things are allowed on paleo. Think plants and animals plus a few modern day comforts like maple syrup, grain free flour, and more.

Folks on paleo enjoy plenty of quality animal protein, with a big emphasis on sourcing. Healthy fats like coconut oil, avocado oil, olive oil and animal fats. All the vegetables, including tubers. Fruit, nuts, seeds and of course the ever-popular paleo treats.

While it is advised to stick to plants and animals, most folks enjoy the occasional cake, cookie, stuffed sweet potato, bacon wrapped dates and other deliciously indulgent paleo meal.

Paleo is not a low-calorie diet. It is organically lower in carbs than the Standard American Diet (SAD) and eliminates gluten and dairy. This shift from SAD, which includes a lot of processed foods and about 500 grams of carbs per day, to paleo which is based on whole foods, and is naturally around 150-200 grams of carbs per day, along with the elimination of gluten and dairy (the two most common inflammatory foods), is why folks feel AMAZING when they make the switch.

Also, on the paleo diet, cane sugar and other forms of processed sugar are not allowed. Most folks severely cut their sugar intake on paleo and use coconut palm sugar, honey and maple syrup but in MUCH smaller amounts.

Once you ditch processed foods (boxed, canned, frozen) you're eliminating a slew of filler ingredients, from binders, starches, various form of sugar, artificial coloring and flavors and preservatives.

KETO AKA KETOGENIC DIET

Ketogenic diets have been used in the medical field for decades to treat epilepsy! They are well researched, which I think is one reason why their popularity is growing so fast. Folks figured out that being in ketosis is not only beneficial for epileptics but great for all of us. Our bodies and especially our brains LOVE using ketones as fuel.

There are a lot of emerging studies which show ketogenic diets helping people with a number of diseases from cancer to Alzheimer's... and this is only the beginning!

Being in ketosis means that your body is using fat for fuel. The body can create energy from two sources: carbohydrates (sugar) or fat (which are metabolized into ketones in the liver). If neither of these are present the body will then break down protein into glucose (sugar), but we don't want that.

That is why the keto diet, while very similar to the paleo diet, has one big difference… MOST of your caloric intake will be from fat. 70-80% to be exact.

Not 70-80% of your food… just your calories, and fat is VERY HIGH in calories, so it's really not THATTTT much. Yup, that's right, you don't need to eat bacon wrapped butter to go keto. Moderate protein intake, about 15-20% and low carb, 10-5%. The macros vary from person to person.

"Protein is a goal; Carbs are a limit. Fat is the lever" -Keto Gains

A balanced keto diet looks a lot like paleo, except swap that sweet potato for an avocado. If you avoid starchy vegetables, fruit and nuts, it will be super easy to get into ketosis. As Mark Sisson says "you're not going to carb load on broccoli!"

When you eat a diet rich in fatty animal proteins with plenty of non-starchy vegetables your body will deplete its glycogen stores (which is usually about 2,000 calories). Once those are gone the body will begin to metabolize fat for energy!

The super cool thing is that when not enough dietary fat is present, a fat adapted person will then use stored body fat for fuel. Yes, you read that right. Your liver can metabolize stored body fat for energy!

Benefits of being in ketosis also include sustained energy levels, no sugar cravings, reduced appetite and mental clarity. Because on keto your body is now privy to endless energy (over 80,000 calories of fat stored in your body) you don't get energy crashes.

When the body uses glycogen (sugar/carbs) for fuel it burns through them very fast so you feel the need to eat for hunger or energy every few hours. The transition from sugar burner to fat burner can be rough, this is the infamous keto flu. It goes away eventually. Taking electrolytes or drinking salt water tends to help.

On keto folks often report being able to go 6+ hours between meals, and a lot of people take on intermittent fasting, where they only eat in small windows and fast 16+ hours a day. I don't recommend taking this on until you are fully fat adapted and comfortable with your ketogenic lifestyle. Baby steps. Set yourself up for success.

Some folks eat dairy on keto, hell, some folks eat gluten on keto. There are a lot of ways to keto. With the goal of eating so low carb your body goes into ketosis there are MANY ways to get there.

The reason eating good fats like avocado, coconut, olive oil and grass-fed butter are important on keto is because these nutritious fats are anti-inflammatory. Think of them as a clean fuel. While processed fats like canola and seed-based oils are like burning fossil fuels. Lots of free radicals and by-products that create a toxic environment in your body.

Bonus: good fats like coconut, grass-fed butter and ghee are rich in medium chain triglycerides (MCT) which go straight to the liver to be processed into ketones, instant energy!

IN A NUT SHELL...

If you're interested in a keto diet to reverse inflammation or lose weight, I high recommend starting with an elimination diet. At least a month of removing all inflammatory foods from your diet. Add them back in one at a time. Log all results.

From there you can transition in to keto or paleo and or a mix of both with all the information YOU need about YOUR body.

Remember, change takes time. Transitioning into this lifestyle, keto, paleo or AIP will be a HUGE change that will affect every aspect of your life. Give yourself grace. Don't compare your day one to someone else's chapter 10. Remember we are all different, each of us with a unique physical and emotional history that will play into how fast we see results.

KETOGENIC DIET AND HASHIMOTO'S

It can be difficult to determine how to use a ketogenic diet for Hashimoto's because most studies focus on how keto diets can affect appetite and weight loss, as well as specific conditions such as type 2 diabetes, rather than the impact on thyroid function.

One important thing to mention is that traditional ketogenic diets use copious amounts of dairy for the fat component, (especially cheeses!), and we know that dairy can be a trigger for Hashimoto's. The use of MCT or coconut oil for a fat source, may be more of a thyroid friendly approach.

If followed mindfully, by removing common reactive foods, including gluten, dairy, soy, and grains, the ketogenic diet can be a very nourishing diet for Hashimoto's. Removing these foods, in addition to sugar sources, contributes to the healing benefits of the ketogenic diet.

People with autoimmune thyroid conditions, however, oftentimes need additional support beyond a standard ketogenic diet, and may find that they need to eliminate other commonly reactive foods, including nuts, nightshades, and eggs. (You can learn more about this in my article on common food sensitivities in those with Hashimoto's.)

Some studies that have looked at the impact of low-carbohydrate diets on T3 and T4 thyroid hormones, as well as thyroid antibodies, show mixed results.

For example, in a 2016 study that looked at the effects of low-carbohydrate diet therapy in people with autoimmune thyroid conditions, 180 people with Hashimoto's were randomized, and a control group ate a low-calorie, low-carbohydrate diet with food restrictions and guidelines.

Their diet contained 12-15 percent carbohydrates, 50-60 percent protein, and 25-30 percent fats. In addition to eating only lean parts of red and white meat, and fish with veggie-rich meals, those on the study diet also eliminated eggs, legumes, dairy products, bread, pasta, fruit, rice, and goitrogens.

After just 21 days, all the patients in the study group showed a significant decrease in their thyroid antibody levels. Based on the way this study was conducted, however, it's difficult to tell whether the carb restriction, removal of highly reactive foods (gluten, dairy, soy, eggs), or all of the above, played a role in improving patient outcomes. (You can read more about my analysis of this study here.)

In another study, the effects of a ketogenic diet on the thyroid of 120 children with epilepsy were monitored for one year. Free T3, T4, and TSH levels were measured at 1, 3, 6, and 12 month intervals. The normal rate of hypothyroidism among preadolescent children is roughly 1 in 1250; however, as a part of this study, 1 in 6 of the children became hypothyroid and required thyroid replacement therapy. It was ultimately concluded that children undergoing a ketogenic diet to treat epilepsy should be closely monitored for thyroid dysfunction.

It's important to consider that diet is not a one-size-fits-all approach to healing, and that it should be individualized to our own needs.

The Keto Foods and Grocery List

Ketogenic foods are foods which are low in carbohydrate, high in fat and lower in protein.

A general list of these foods includes both animal and plant based foods, but they are all real, whole foods such as:

- Meats, poultry and seafood in any form, preferably grass fed or wild caught (for instance, imitation crabmeat is not wild caught and has sugar and starch in it.) You can choose from beef, pork, chicken, turkey, shellfish, fish and the higher the fat content of the meat, the better. Dark meat thighs or better options than lean chicken breast, for example.
- Eggs, in any form. Deviled eggs make great snacks, and eggs in many forms are typically are a breakfast foundation food. Quiche, scrambled eggs, omelets, poached eggs, hard boiled eggs are all good choices.
- Natural Fats: I believe one should only eat real, organic fats like butter, cream and coconut oil, but if you want to include commercial mayonnaise, vegetable oils and olive oil, you can. However, I do advise leaning toward butter, olive oil and coconut oil, and limiting your intake of refined vegetable oils (soybean, canola, safflower, sunflower or corn oil) as they are high in Omega 6 fatty acids and can contribute to a long list of health issues associated with inflammation.
- Green leafy vegetables such as lettuce, spinach, kale, collards, cucumbers and high fiber cruciferous vegetables such as broccoli, cauliflower and cabbage. You'll need to track how much of the sweeter vegetables you eat (tomatoes, peppers, summer squash) because these are higher in carb. A whole plate of tomatoes will quickly put you over your carb limit.

This low carb food list of foods are also allowed on a ketogenic diet.

Cooking is a Big Part of Eating Well

As you look over these lists, you'll notice that these foods are close to their natural state. This means they require cooking to prepare them properly. This is an important point to remember.

Eating a healthy ketogenic diet means you'll need to spend more time in the kitchen. Most processed foods are convenient of course, but they are also full of sugar and starch.

If you are switching to a ketogenic foods diet for health reasons, giving up processed food and learning to cook for yourself are major steps on the path to better health.

However, If You Really Hate to Cook

If you don't know how to cook, and don't want to learn, there are ways to still eat ketogenic foods. There are lots of restaurants which have low carb options on the menus, and in a pinch, you can get a fast food hamburger and just avoid eating the bread.

There are restaurants which offer low carb choices, or gluten free menus which are usually lower in carb. The trick is to plan ahead. Usually, you can get the menu of a restaurant on the internet, then you'll have time to really look at it and make a wise choice without the pressure of the waiter or waitress waiting for your decision.

Your best bet for staying on plan is to order some sort of roasted or broiled meat and a salad with the dressing on the side. Or order a salad as a meal, such as a big Caesar with broiled chicken on top. Just be mindful of vinagrette dressings, they usually have a lot of sugar in them. Creamy dressings are usually higher in fat and lower in carb.

There are also grocery stores which offer pre-cooked foods such as roasted chickens, steamed shrimp, beef brisket, etc. Through in a salad with some full fat dressing and you have a keto meal.

However, I think that part of the journey toward better health is developing a habit of caring for yourself, and I can't think of a better way than to be able to make a delicious meal out of real, whole foods for yourself.

THE DAIRY FREE KETO

You May Have Lactose Intolerance and Not Even Realize It

Even if you don't think dairy is a problem for you, you may still have some form of lactose intolerance or dairy protein allergy. In fact, you may be struggling to break down lactose (milk sugar) without realizing it.

This is because, the majority of the human population — approximately 65 percent — has a reduced ability to digest lactose after infancy. More specifically, if you are of East Asian, West African, Arab, Jewish, Greek, and Italian descent, then you are highly likely to have some form of lactose intolerance.

Conversely, the prevalence of lactose intolerance is lowest in people with ancestors who depended on unfermented milk products as a primary food source. For this reason, only about 5 percent of people of Northern European descent are lactose intolerant.

In other words, if your ancestors didn't drink a lot of milk, then you probably have some form of lactose intolerance. This happens because our bodies stop producing the lactase enzyme that helps break down lactose (milk sugar) after being weaned off of breastfeeding.

Why does this happen?

Throughout our evolutionary history, we rarely encountered lactose unless it was from our mother's milk. Thus, our bodies produce lactase during our first years of life to help us digest the breastmilk and divert that energy elsewhere once we start eating solid food.)

Without the lactase enzyme, lactose is metabolized by gut bacteria, which can cause stomach upset, flatulence, diarrhea, bloating, nausea, and a host of familiar but unwelcome gastrointestinal symptoms. But don't worry, this isn't life threatening — it is just annoying and can make life difficult and unpleasant.

If you find that you feel worse after eating a dairy-heavy meal, then you may have some degree of lactose intolerance. To verify if you actually do struggle with lactose, you can get a breath test or a blood glucose test after drinking a lactose-rich drink, but these are much more time intensive and cost more money.

The simplest way to test for lactose intolerance is by mixing lactose powder with water and drinking it to see if digestive issues emerge. To do this, start with 25 grams of lactose first thing in the morning or 3 hours after your last meal. After drinking the lactose drink, pay attention to how you feel.

Take notice if one or more of these symptoms develop:

- abdominal cramps
- bloating

- diarrhea
- stomach or intestinal pain
- gassiness (burping or flatulence)
- indigestion

If one or more of these symptoms occur after drinking the lactose-drink, then you have some degree of lactose intolerance. The severity of the symptoms is a good indicator as to how well your body can handle lactose-containing foods.

For those who have minor symptoms during the lactose powder test, you can probably handle the amount of lactose you'll be getting with the ketogenic diet. On the other hand, if the lactose causes some serious digestive distress, here are some things that you can do:

- Limit your dairy intake and eat mostly low-lactose dairy products like hard cheese and butter.
- Take a lactase enzyme supplement right before eating dairy-heavy meals.
- Eliminate all dairy from your diet by following the recipes in this book

The good news is that the ketogenic diet tends to be much lower in lactose than any other dairy-containing diet, so you may only get minor side effects with some keto meals. However, if your body is struggling with low-lactose dairy products like butter or cheddar cheese, then you may have a dairy allergy or an intolerance to dairy protein, not lactose intolerance.

Here are some strategies for those who react negatively to dairy in some way:

1. Eliminate it from your keto diet entirely.
2. Reduce your dairy consumption to a point where you don't notice negative effects.
3. Take a lactase enzyme with your dairy-rich meal if you are only lactose intolerant.
4. Limit yourself to specific forms of dairy that you don't react to.

At this point, however, you may be wondering if it is even possible to be on a dairy-free ketogenic diet. After all, most of the recipes call for butter, heavy cream, or some form of cheese.

Yes, this is true, but it doesn't mean that you won't be able to eliminate all dairy from your diet. In fact, once you know what to avoid, what keto recipes to make, and what dairy alternatives you can use, you'll be able to live a dairy-free lifestyle just as easily as it is to live a dairy-filled lifestyle.

Things to avoid on Dairy Free Diet

Here is a comprehensive list of what you should avoid if you want to be completely dairy-free:

- Butter, butter fat, butter oil, butter acid, butter esters

- Buttermilk
- Casein, casein hydrolysate, rennet casein and caseinates (in all forms)
- Cheese (all animal milk based cheeses)
- Cottage cheese
- Heavy Cream
- Curds
- Custard and pudding
- Diacetyl
- Half-and-half
- Lactalbumin, lactalbumin phosphate, and lactoferrin
- Lactose, lactulose, and tagatose
- Milk (in all forms including condensed, derivative, dry, evaporated, goat's milk and milk from other animals, low-fat, malted, milk fat, non-fat, powder, protein, skimmed, solids, whole)
- Milk-based protein powders
- Sour cream, sour cream solids, and sour milk solids
- Whey (in all forms)
- Yogurt (in all forms)

Other possible sources of dairy proteins or lactose:

- Artificial butter flavor
- Baked goods
- Caramel candies
- Chocolate
- Lactic acid starter culture and other bacterial cultures
- Luncheon meat, hot dogs, and sausages that use the milk protein casein as a binder. Also, deli meat slicers are often used for both meat and cheese products, leading to dairy contamination.
- Margarine
- Nisin
- Non-dairy products that contain casein
- Nougat
- Shellfish may be dipped in milk to reduce the fishy odor. (Ask the seller if they do this when buying shellfish.)
- Brands of tuna fish that contain casein
- Some specialty products made with milk substitutes (e.g., soy, nut, or rice-based dairy alternatives) are manufactured on equipment shared with milk.
- Many restaurants put butter on grilled steaks to add extra flavor.
- Some medications contain milk protein.

Although not all of these products will contain lactose or milk proteins, it is important to be mindful of everything you are buying and eating. Make sure you read food labels carefully and ask questions if you're ever unsure about an item's ingredients.

Keep in mind, however, that while you are on the ketogenic diet, you will not encounter many of the ingredients/foods on the two lists above.

Foods to eat on Dairy Free Keto Diet

Now that you know what to avoid on the dairy-free keto diet, here is what you can eat:

1. Animal fats and plant-based oils. Avoid all fats that are derived from dairy and stick with plant-based oils like coconut oil, MCT oil, and olive oil and animal fats like lard, tallow, and duck fat.
2. Red meat, poultry, and seafood. Try to stick with organic, pasture-raised, and 100% grass-fed meat and wild caught fish where possible.
3. Low-carb vegetables. Stick with above ground vegetables, leaning toward leafy/green produce. Check out our low-carb vegetable guide to find out exactly what vegetables to eat on keto and how many carbs are in each one.
4. Low-carb fruits. Although most fruits are not keto-friendly, there are a handful that make a great addition to the ketogenic diet. Some examples of keto-friendly fruits are avocados, berries, and some citrus fruits. For a more detailed guide on what fruits you should and shouldn't eat on keto, click here.
5. Nuts and seeds. Eat nuts and seeds in moderation as some contain a decent amount of carbs. Try to use fattier nuts like macadamias, pecans, and almonds.
6. Dairy alternatives. There are plenty dairy alternatives that you can use to replace common keto foods like heavy cream, cheese, sour cream, half and half, and yogurt.

The easiest way to cut dairy products out of your diet is by looking for dairy-free keto recipes and making a shopping list based on the ingredients. This way you will know for sure that you won't end up buying any products that contain dairy, while simultaneously ensuring that you will have plenty of delicious keto-friendly food to eat.

Once you get the hang of dairy-free shopping and cooking, feel free to experiment with different dairy substitutions to make your favorite dairy-heavy keto recipes into 100% dairy-free meals.

How to Implement the Dairy-Free Ketogenic Diet Meal Plan Properly?

With this dairy-free ketogenic meal plan template, you'll be able to map out what you need to get from the grocery store for a week's worth of meals while guaranteeing that you won't be consuming any dairy products at all.

I also tried to put together the meal plan so that you only have to make each recipe once a week and eat the leftover servings a couple of days later. This way, you can save time and money while you implement the dairy-free ketogenic diet.

Although I suggest how many servings you should eat, this doesn't mean that they will meet your specific calorie and macronutrient needs. Make sure you use the calorie breakdowns on the meals to guide your decision of how much to eat. Your meals should be big enough to meet your calorie, protein, and fat needs for the day without needing any snacks or dessert.

What do you do if you there are one or two dairy ingredients in your favorite keto recipe?

Use a dairy alternative.

Here are keto-friendly dairy alternatives for the most common dairy products that you will encounter on the ketogenic diet.

Common dairy substitutions on a ketogenic diet.

HOW TO REPLACE WHOLE MILK

The most reliable whole milk alternative is coconut milk. In recipes, you can substitute coconut milk in for regular whole milk in a 1 to 1 ratio.

However, make sure the coconut milk you are getting doesn't have any added sugar or carbs.

If the recipe calls for a lower fat milk, then use light coconut milk. Conversely, when the recipe calls for whole milk, use the richest coconut milk you can find (I prefer Aroy-d 100% Coconut Milk).

DAIRY-FREE HEAVY CREAM SUBSTITUTIONS

There are three effective heavy cream alternatives that I know of:

- Coconut Cream. You can either allow a can of full-fat coconut milk to settle (about 1/2 hour) and scoop the cream off the top or purchase coconut cream online or from the store. To substitute cream in recipes, use equal parts coconut cream for the dairy cream. This will work particularly well in sauces for seafood and poultry.
- High-Protein Soy Cream Alternative. Blend Silken Tofu until smooth. This pureed tofu can be substituted for heavy cream using a 1:1 ratio. It works as an excellent cream substitute when a thickener is needed in sauces and soups. Choose medium firm or firm varieties for a thicker "cream".
- Milk + Oil Heavy Cream Replacement. Blend 2/3 cup of soy or rice milk with 1/3 cup of oil (extra light olive oil is best for cooking). This will replace 1 cup of heavy cream for your recipes. Keep in mind, however, that it will not whip.

How to Replace Sour Cream

- Although these don't taste exactly like sour cream, they do the trick:
- Vegan Yogurt. Use a plain unflavored and unsweetened variety of dairy-free yogurt as a 1:1 sour cream substitute. Works best in dips and salad dressings.

- Soy Sour Cream. Blend up some firm Silken Tofu for a wonderful sour cream like consistency. Use as a 1:1 sour cream substitute for more savory dishes.
- Nut-based Sour Cream. For a delicious soy-free sour cream alternative, you can make your own sour cream using cashews or sunflower seeds as the base. Google search "cashew sour cream" to find a recipe that works for you.

DAIRY-FREE BUTTER ALTERNATIVES

- For frying, use coconut oil, olive oil, or ghee (a butter product that has all of the dairy proteins taken out).
- For a buttery spread (for keto breads or muffins), use coconut butter, nut butter, or seed butter.
- For baking, use coconut butter (or coconut manna), a vegan butter (that doesn't contain hydrogenated oils), or ghee in the same way that you would use butter.
- You can also use olive oil for baking as well. If a recipe calls for 1/2 cup butter, try using 1/3 cup oil instead (this may require a bit of experimentation).

GROCERY LIST FOR DIARY AND GLUTEN-FREE DIET

Veggies:

All Greens like: Parsley, Cilantro, Broccoli, Bok Choy, Spinach, Green lettuce, Cabbage (Green or Red), Celery, Fresh Dill, Avocados, Brussels sprouts, Bean Sprouts, Asparagus, Snow Peas, Cucumber, Cauliflower, Zucchinis, Fresh green onions, Yellow or Red Raw onions.

Ferments:

Fermented Sauerkraut, Fermented Gut Shots, Fermented Kimchi

Poultry: (Organic and Grass Fed if you can)

- Chicken Thighs, Wings, Legs, Grounded Chicken, Chicken Bone Broth
- Turkey Legs, Grounded Turkey, Turkey Breast, Whole Turkey, Turkey Bacon (Nitrate free), Turkey Sausage.

Beef of all kinds (make sure that they are Grass Fed), Roast beef, Baby Back Ribs, Steak all cuts and Beef Bone Broths

Pork: Bacon (Nitrate free), Pork chops, Tenderloin, Ground Pork, Pork Roast, Ham (unglazed)

Seafood: Bass, Cod, Salmon, Haddock, Halibut, Shrimp, Sole, Trout (Make sure that the seafood you eat is WILD) *Never eat Farmed Fish avoid at all cost*

Sauce: Apple cider vinegar, Yellow or brown mustard, Lakanto Maple syrup (Keto Friendly), Lemon juice, Lime juice, Ranch (my homemade Hemp ranch dressing, recipe under files), Sugar free Ketchup, Low carb Salsa.

Liquids: (Nondairy) Hemp milk, Coconut milk, Almond milk, Herbal Tea, Herbal Teas like (Dandelion, Green Tea, Chamomile, Pau D'Arcy), Coffee (Organic), Protein Powders from (Sun Warrior, Perfect Keto, Equip Food)

Spices: Paprika, Garlic powder, Oregano, Onion powder, Pink Himalayan Salt, Turmeric, Allspice, Chili powder, Cumin, Cinnamon ((Black pepper does contain carbs)) ---(Make sure your spice rack is Organic)

Fruits: Blackberries, Blueberries, Raspberries, Strawberries, Olives (Organic Greek Olives green or black)

Fats and Oils: Vegan / Soy Free Butter by: Earth Balance, Bacon Fat, Coconut oil, MCT Oil or the Powder by: Perfect Keto, Duck Fat / Lard, Mayo Vegan, Olive oil, Avocado Oil, Beef bone broth/Chicken bone broth, Coconut Cream.

Cooking and Baking: Coconut Flour, Almond Flour, Coconut Flakes, Coconut Meat, Coconut Water, Flax Meal, Flax seeds, Chia seeds, Cocoa powder, Nutritional Yeast, Macadamia Nuts, Brazilian Nuts, Cacao Nibs, Pistachios, Pumpkin Seeds, All Seeds.

Sweeteners: Erythritol, Stevia drops, Stevia Powder, Stevia Flavors, Vanilla Extract (any extracts are fine depending on your sweet tooth)

SEASONING AND CONDIMENT

Italian Seasoning

Total Time: 5 Min

Yield: 4 Teaspoons (Or 1 1/3 Tablespoons)

This delicious Italian seasoning recipe is simple to make at home!

Ingredients:

- 1 1/2 teaspoons dried oregano
- 1 teaspoon dried marjoram
- 1 teaspoon dried thyme
- 1/2 teaspoon dried basil
- 1/2 teaspoon dried rosemary
- 1/2 teaspoon dried sage

Instructions

1. Whisk all seasonings together in a bowl until combined. Use immediately or store in a sealed container.

Ketchup!

This tastes as authentic as it looks and is super easy to make once you have all the ingredients at hand!

Ingredients:

- ½ c packed boiled carrots
- 2 T apple cider vinegar or lemon juice
- ½ tsp salt
- 1 tsp tamarind paste
- 3T water
- 2 large dates (30g)
- splash of beet juice (for color).

Instructions

Soak the dates in the water while you prepare the rest of the ingredients and add all to a high speed blender and puree. Ta-dah! Perfect ketchup- seriously, it's that easy!!!!

Creamy Mayo

Total time: 8 mins

Recipe type: Condiments

Serves: 2/3 cup

Creamy, tangy and the closest to real mayo that I've tasted.

Ingredients

- 1/3 cup avocado oil (Olive will work fine as well, but will have an olive tint and flavor.)
- tbsp palm shortening
- 1 tsp lemon juice
- 1/4 tsp salt

Instructions

2 Place all ingredients in small mixing bowl.

3 Beat on high with handheld mixer for 7 minutes.

4 Store in jar or airtight container in refrigerator. (Keeps well for long periods.)

BREAKFAST

Breakfast Roll in a Bowl -

Prep Time: 10 minutes ||**Cook Time:** 13 minutes

Servings: 6

Calories: 304

This Healthy Roll in a Bowl has all of the great flavor of Rolls, but it's an Easy One Pan Meal without the grain wrapper!

Ingredients

- 1 1/2 lbs ground beef (turkey or chicken or game meat may also be used)
- 2 med onions (finely chopped / minced)
- 1 1/2 Tbsp coconut oil
- 1 1/2 tsp ginger (powdered)
- 1 tsp garlic granules (or 4 cloves garlic, minced)
- 1/2 tsp salt (or to taste)
- 1/16 tsp maple syrup or honey
- 1/3 cup beef broth
- 9 cups shredded cabbage
- 1 1/2 cups shredded carrot
- 4 tsp coconut aminos
- Green onion for garnish (optional)

Instructions

1. Place meat in large pan and cook until browned.
2. On medium high heat, add the onions and coconut oil. Cook until lightly browned.
3. Reduce heat to medium.
4. Add spices, honey, and broth to the pan and stir well.
5. Add the cabbage and stir to coat.
6. Cook, stirring frequently until the cabbage slightly wilts.
7. Add carrots and cook for 2-3 minutes until soft.
8. Add coconut aminos to taste and adjust flavorings as desired.
9. Serve plain or over rice or cauliflower rice.
10. Garnish with green onions if desired.

Calories: 304kcal | Carbohydrates: 13.2g | Protein: 37.1g | Fat: 10.7g | Saturated Fat: 3.2g | Cholesterol: 101mg | Sodium: 574mg | Potassium: 805mg | Fiber: 4.2g | Sugar: 6.4g | Calcium: 50mg | Iron: 22.1mg

Aian Garlic Beef noodles recipe

Prep Time: 10 minutes||Cook Time: 20 minutes

Yield: 2 servings

Category: Entree

Ingredients

- 1/2 onion, sliced
- 10 oz (300 g) beef, cubed or sliced
- 2 Tablespoons avocado oil (or coconut oil)
- 2 Tablespoons coconut aminos
- 10 cloves garlic, diced
- 1 large chunk of fresh ginger, diced
- 2 Tablespoons cilantro, chopped (for garnish)
- 1 zucchini, shredded, or use a pack of shirataki noodles

Instructions

1. Saute the onion slices in the avocado oil.
2. Add in the beef cubes or slices.
3. Add in the coconut aminos
4. Cook until the beef is tender (place a lid on the pan to cook it if it needs longer).

5. Add in the diced garlic and ginger. Cook for 5 minutes longer.
6. Divide the shredded zucchini or the shirataki noodles between 2 plates. Top with the beef saute.
7. Garnish with the chopped cilantro and serve.

Calories: 620 Sugar: 0 g Fat: 50 g Carbohydrates: 5 g Fiber: 0 g Protein: 37 g

Adobo Chicken Burgers

Prep Time: 5 mins // Cook Time: 10 mins

Yield: 6 burgers

Ingredients

- Coconut oil
- 1 tsp garlic powder
- 1 tsp onion powder
- 1 tsp turmeric
- 1.5 tsp dried oregano
- 1lb ground chicken or turkey
- 1/4 cup red onion, finely diced
- 1 large handful of spinach, finely chopped (approximately 1 cup)
- 1/2 tsp himalayan pink salt + more to taste

Instructions

1. Preheat oil over medium heat in a large cast iron skillet.
2. Mix ground chicken, red onion, spinach, and seasoning in a large bowl until well combined. Divide into 6 equal portions and form burger patties.
3. Cook burgers for 4-5 minutes per side or until it reaches an internal temperature of 165 degrees.
4. Serve warm over roasted vegetables, a bed of spinach, or in a lettuce wrap.

Thai Meatballs

Time: 20 minutes

Serves: 4

Ingredients:

- 1 pound ground grass fed beef (pork or lamb or chicken would also be good)
- 2 T grated fresh ginger (I store mine in the freezer)
- 20 mint leaves
- 1/3 cup mixed herbs – equal parts parsley & cilantro – chopped
- 1 spring onion – green part only – chopped
- 1 lime juiced + 1 lime for squeezing at the table
- 1 t fish sauce
- 1/2 t salt
- coconut or olive oil for cooking

Instructions

1. Finely chop all the herbs – make a big pile of all of them on the chopping board and chop away
2. Grate the ginger
3. Combine mix-ins – herbs, ginger, salt, fish sauce, lime juice in a bowl
4. Add the mix-ins to the ground beef
5. Form into small meatballs (1 inch)

6. Heat coconut or olive oil in a large skillet over medium heat and place meatballs in the pan
7. Cook for 4-5 minutes then turn and cook another 4 minutes, then move them around in the pan for another 3-4 minutes until all sides are brown and they are cooked through (remove one to test the doneness)
8. Serve with a roasted veggies, a simple salad, or on zoodles
9. Extra lime wedges for squeezing over the meatballs is also a good idea

Herbed Beef Breakfast Patties

Prep Time: 5 mins || Cook time: 10 mins.

These flavorful beef patties are a great option for breakfast or even a fun option for burgers!

Ingredients

- 2 lbs grass-fed ground beef
- 1.5 tbsp dried ground sage
- 3 tsp dried marjoram
- 2 tsp granulated garlic
- 2 tsp granulated onion
- 1 tsp ground ginger
- 1 tsp finely ground unrefined salt

Instructions

1. Combine all the seasonings in a small bowl and mix.
2. Add ground beef to a large bowl. To avoid over-working the meat while mixing in the seasoning, spread the meat across the bottom of the bowl and sprinkle with seasoning. Turn meat over and sprinkle again, gently working into the meat.
3. Heat a large frying pan over medium heat. While the pan is heating, divide meat into 12 to 16 portions. Roll each into a ball and flatten into a disc.
4. Fry the patties, working in batches as needed, until cooked through and both sides are well-browned and slightly crispy, about 10 minutes total.
5. Note: If you ground beef is very lean you may need to add a small amount of fat to the pan just before adding the patties.
6. Serve and enjoy! Store leftovers in an airtight container in the fridge and reheat in a 350F oven for about 10 minutes.

Italian Tuna Mousse

Prep Time: 5 mins || Total Time: 5 mins

Yield: 1 cup

This 'Italian Tuna Mousse' turns humble tuna salad into a dip/ spread you can be proud to serve at your next gathering. The tuna, avocado & olive oil all provide you with some satiating healthy fats, the hidden spinach adds an iron boost and the lime and oregano provide the flavors of the Mediterranean.

Ingredients

- 1/4 cup baby spinach
- 2 T parsley
- 1 t dried oregano
- 1 lime – juiced
- 1/2 of a medium haas avocado
- 1 can tuna (packed in olive oil) – *See Note Below

Instructions

1. place spinach, parsley, oregano, lime juice, avocado, oil from tuna & 1/4 of the tuna in a food processor and blend til smooth
2. place remaining tuna in a bowl and flake apart
3. add avocado mixture and stir til well combined
4. serve with veggies (carrots, celery, cucumber) and plantain chips

**NOTE ON TUNA –

My preference for this is olive oil packed Italian tuna as it has a milder taste and less fishy smell. If you can't find this kind of tuna, it's ok to use whatever AIP compliant tuna you have and drain it well if packed in water and add 1T of a good quality olive oil to the avocado mixture.

Breakfast Bowl with Shrimp and Bacon

Prep Time: 10 || Cook Time: 10

Yield: 2

Breakfast

Ingredients

- 1 large broccoli crown
- 1 small head of cauliflower
- 1 small vidalia onion
- 2 garlic cloves
- 1 cup water (or bone broth)
- 1/2 tsp pink Himalaya salt
- 2 slices bacon
- 6–10 shrimp, depending on size
- 1 tsp Himalayan salt salt
- 1 tbsp coconut aminos
- 1 tsp dried cilantro

Instructions

1. Place bacon on a sheet pan and put it in the oven.
2. Set to 375F.
3. In the mean time, chop up broccoli, cauliflower, onion and garlic.
4. Add to your pressure cooker.
5. Add in the water and 1/2 salt. Close and set to the vegetable setting, or on low for 7 minutes..
6. In a bowl toss together the shrimp and salt.
7. When the oven reaches 375F, check on the bacon.
8. When it's almost done, add the shrimp to the same sheet pan.
9. Roast it all together for 5 minutes. Open the oven, give the sheet pan a shake.
10. Roast another 2-3 minutes.
11. By now the pressure cooker should be done with the vegetables.
12. Add all the veggies and half the liquid in to a blender, and puree until smooth.
13. You can add the remaining liquid if you want it less thick.
14. Serve some vegetable puree in a bowl, you will have a lot left over!
15. Remove shrimp and bacon from oven.
16. Chop up shrimp and bacon carefully and serve over vegetable puree.
17. Drizzle bacon fat over your dish, then coconut aminos and lastly cilantro.

Serving Size: 1/2 Recipe, Calories: 203, Fat: 4g, Carbohydrates: 19g, Fiber: 10g, Protein: 42g

keto Breakfast Stack

Prep Time: 15 minutes || **Cook Time:** 15 minutes

Yield: 2 servings

Ingredients

- 4 slices bacon (**use AIP-compliant bacon if you're staying AIP**)
- 1/4 lb (110 g) ground pork
- 1/4 lb (110 g) ground chicken
- 2 teaspoons (2 g) Italian seasoning
- 1 teaspoon (5 g) salt
- 2 large flat mushrooms (like portobello)
- 1 avocado, sliced

Instructions

1. Cook the bacon until crispy. Leave the fat in the pan.
2. Mix together the ground pork, chicken, Italian seasoning and salt in a bowl and form 4 thin patties.
3. Pan-fry the patties in the bacon fat.
4. Then pan-fry the mushrooms.
5. Put together your keto breakfast stack with the mushrooms on the bottom, then 2 thin patties, then 3 slices of avocado, and top it with the slices of bacon. Serve with the rest of the avocado slices.

Net Carbs: 5 g

Calories: 680 Sugar: 2 g Fat: 54 g Carbohydrates: 13 g Fiber: 8 g Protein: 38 g

Coconut Yogurt Berry Parfait Recipe

Prep Time: 5 minutes || Cook Time: 0 minutes

Yield: 2 servings

Ingredients

- 1 pot (120 ml) coconut yogurt
- 1 strawberry, diced small
- 2 raspberries
- 1 teaspoon coconut flakes
- 1/2 teaspoon cacao nibs (optional)

Instructions

1. Carefully spoon 1 tablespoon of coconut yogurt into each jar or glass. Tap the jar or glass against your hand to ensure it falls the bottom of the container.
2. Add a layer of diced strawberries, coconut flakes, and any other toppings you want (e.g., cacao nibs).
3. Add another tablespoon of coconut yogurt on top.
4. Place a raspberry on top of the parfait.
5. Serve for breakfast or as a snack.

Calories: 40 Sugar: 3 g Fat: 2 g Carbohydrates: 3 g Fiber: 0 g Protein: 2 g

Spinach & Mushroom Alfredo with Bacon!

Prep Time: 20mins ||Cook Time: 20 mins

Yield: 4 servings

Serving Size: 1/4 Recipe

Ingredients

Noodles

- 1/2 spaghetti squash, roasted (I halve and roast at 400F for 35 minutes)
- shirataki noodles, or zoodles for lower carb

THE FIXINGS

- 4 slices sugar free, nightshade free bacon
- 4 cups raw spinach
- 2 cup sliced, cremini or baby bella mushrooms
- 4 garlic cloves
- 1 sprig fresh basil

THE SAUCE

- 1 head cauliflower, about 3 cups diced
- 2 small onions, 1 cup diced
- 2 garlic cloves
- 1/2 cup coconut milk
- 1/2 cup bone broth
- 2 tablespoons Red Boat No.49 fish sauce
- 1 tablespoon red win vinegar
- 1 tsp oregano
- 1 tsp salt
- 1 tbsp olive oil

Instructions

1. If you haven't done so already, roast your spaghetti squash, halve, place meat side down on a sheet pan and roast until hard shell can be pierced by a fork.
2. About 35 minutes at 400F.
3. Next prepare Alfredo sauce: dice cauliflower, onion, garlic. Heat olive oil in a large pot, add in garlic, & onion. Saute on high for 6 minutes, stirring often until tender.
4. Then add in cauliflower, stir well. Add in salt, oregano, broth & coconut milk.
5. Stir well. Lower heat to medium-low.

6. Cover with a tight-fitting lid.
7. Let it cook simmering until the cauliflower is very tender, about 15 minutes.
8. Transfer all of it to a blender, carefully!
9. Add in the fish sauce and vinegar. Blend until smooth.
10. Taste, adjust salt as needed.

You can also prepare cauliflower in a pressure cooker, start with saute mode, then close and set to vegetable (for 8 minutes).

TO PREPARE THE DISH: COOK THE BACON FIRST.

1. Lay bacon flat on a cooling rack over sheet pan, and put the pan in a cold oven, then set oven to 350F
2. After it reaches 350F check on bacon, set timer to 8 minutes, check again, cook until crispy.
3. Heat olive oil in a large skillet.
4. Slice garlic cloves & mushrooms.
5. Once skillet is hot add in mushrooms & garlic.
6. Saute in the skillet on high until tender. Sprinkle with a pinch of salt.
7. Add in spinach.
8. Stir and saute until wilted.
9. Add in 1 cup of Alfredo sauce.
10. Stir well & remove from heat.
11. Using a fork, pull out all the meat of one half the spaghetti squash.
12. Add it to the skillet.
13. Chop up crispy bacon & add it to the skillet as well.
14. Garnish with fresh basil.
15. Mix it all up and serve 2 moderate portions, or serve in a generous bowl & chow down!

Avocado, Bacon and Balsamic

Serves: 2

Prep Time: 5 mins || Cook Time: 5 min

Perfect for a snack, or even breakfast.

Ingredients

- 1 avocado
- slices cooked bacon chopped
- 1 teaspoon aged balsamic vinegar to taste
- sea salt to taste

Instructions

1. Halve the avocado and remove pit.
2. Sprinkle with bacon, balsamic vinegar, and sea salt to taste.
3. Serve with a spoon.

Calories: 254kcal | Carbohydrates: 9g | Protein: 4g | Fat: 23g | Saturated Fat: 5g | Cholesterol: 14mg | Sodium: 153mg | Potassium: 530mg | Fiber: 6g | Sugar: 1g | Vitamin A: 145IU | Vitamin C: 10.1mg | Calcium: 12mg | Iron: 0.6mg

Sausage Breakfast Hash

Prep Time: 30 mins || Cook Time: 15 mins.

Serves: 2 servings

Ingredients

- 1lb of pastured ground pork or grass-fed beef
- 1 tsp dried rubbed sage
- 1/2 tsp of dried thyme
- 1/2 tsp onion powder
- 1/4 tsp fine sea salt or to taste
- 1 Tbs. EVOO or fat of choice
- 1 frozen pkg of frozen organic spinach, thawed & drained or several handfuls of fresh
- 1 Leek, coarsely chopped & washed (or you could sub onion)
- 1 container of organic mushrooms, sliced or 1 can of organic mushrooms
- 1 organic squash or zucchini chopped

Instructions

1. Add Seasonings to Pork.
2. Heat Pan to Med Heat.
3. Saute Pork until brown.
4. Add leeks. Cook until tender.
5. Add Mushrooms & Squash & cook until tender
6. Add Spinach & cook until wilted.

Raspberry Coconut Drops

Cook Time:1 hr || Prep Time: 5 mins

Serves: 20

Load up on healthy fats with these keto and AIP Raspberry Coconut Drops made with zero refined sugar.

Ingredients

- 1/2 cup coconut butter
- 1/2 cup coconut oil
- T raspberries
- 1/2 t alcohol-free pure vanilla extract

Instructions

1. Place fresh raspberries on parchment-lined baking dish and set in freezer for one hour or until frozen.
2. Meanwhile, stir coconut butter, coconut oil and vanilla extract in a small pot on medium heat. Stir occasionally to help all ingredients fully melt.
3. Remove the raspberries from the freezer and place in a blender. Pulse several times until a crumbly mixture forms.
4. Add the raspberries to the pot with the coconut butter and stir to incorporate well.
5. Spoon the mixture into the silicone molds. Use a knife to flatten and smooth.
6. Place in the freezer one hour or until the coconut drops are solidified.
7. Remove from the freezer and pop the drops out of the molds to serve.
8. Keep in the refrigerator for up to 10 days or in the freezer for 30 days.

Keto Cottage Pie

Prep Time: 15 minutes || **Cook Time:** 45 minutes

Yield: 4 servings

Ingredients

- 1 head of cauliflower (600 g), broken into florets
- Tablespoons of coconut oil
- 0.25 cup of avocado oil (60 ml), to cook beef with
- 1 medium onion (110 g), finely chopped
- 1.5 lbs of ground beef (675 g)
- 2 carrots (100 g), grated
- 2 Tablespoons of AIP Italian seasoning blend (6 g)
- 2 Tablespoons of fresh parsley (2 g), finely chopped

Instructions

1   Preheat the oven to 350 F (175 C).
2   Steam the cauliflower until fork-tender, about 5 to 10 minutes (depending on the size of the florets). Drain well.

3   In a food processor or blender, combine the cauliflower with the ghee. Season with salt, to taste. Set aside.
4   Meanwhile, add the avocado oil to a large skillet over medium-high heat. Add the onion and saute until translucent, about 4 to 5 minutes.
5   Add the ground beef and carrots to the skillet. Saute until the ground beef is browned, about 8 to 10 minutes.
6   Add the Italian seasoning and parsley to the skillet, stirring well to combine. Season with salt, to taste.
7   Place the beef mixture in the bottom of a greased baking dish (9-inch x 9-inch (23cm x 23cm) or large oval dish would work). Place the reserved cauliflower mash on top of the beef mixture.
8   Place the baking dish in the oven and bake for 30 minutes.
9   Remove from oven and let cool slightly before serving.

Net Carbs: 8 g

Calories: 684 Sugar: 6 g Fat: 57 g Carbohydrates: 13 g Fiber: 5 g Protein: 32 g

Dairy-Free Keto Lemon Fat Bombs

Serves: 10

Prep Time: 60

Ingredients:

- 3/4 cup coconut butter
- 1/4 cup coconut oil
- tablespoons lemon juice
- Zest of 1 lemon
- 1 tablespoon coconut cream (the thick part from a can of coconut milk)
- 1 tablespoon Honey
- 1 teaspoon vanilla powder
- Pinch of salt

Instructions:

1. Place all ingredients in a blender and blend to combine.
2. Line a plate or dish with parchment. Scoop the fat bomb mixture out onto the parchment. Freeze for 30 minutes, or until firm enough to handle without melting.
3. Remove the mixture from the freezer, roll into balls, and chill again in the freezer until set.
4. Enjoy immediately or store covered in the fridge or freezer (freezer storage may require thawing time).

NOTE: coconut butter is the same as coconut mana and coconut concentrate

Calories: 164, Fat: 16.7g, Salt: 23mg, Carbs: 4.6g, Fiber: 3g, Sugar: 1.4g, Sugar Alcohols: 1.2g, Net Carbs: .4g, Protein: 1.3g, Cholesterol: 0mg, Potassium: 10mg, Calcium: 7mg, Iron: 1mg

Guacamole Stuffed Burgers

Prep Time: 10 minutes || Cook Time: 16 minutes

Servings: 4 burgers

Calories: 374kcal

These Whole30 and keto guacamole stuffed burgers are easy to make and packed with flavor. You'll love the taste of tangy guacamole with every bite!

Ingredients

Burger Patties

- 1 lb ground beef preferably grass fed
- 3/4 tsp sea salt
- garlic cloves minced

Guacamole

- 1 medium avocado ripe
- tbsp lime juice
- 1/4 tsp sea salt
- tbsp chopped cilantro

Optional toppings

- Sliced onions
- Lettuce for wrapping

Instructions

1. In a large bowl, place all ingredients for the burger patties and mix together to combine. Be careful not to over-mix.
2. In a separate bowl, mash all ingredients for guacamole together.
3. Divide the burger meat into 4 equal sections.
4. Use your hands to divide each section in half. Flatten each half into similar sized circles, similar in diameter as a burger patty.
5. Add a scoop of guacamole to the center of one circle, and top with the other circle.
6. Pinch the sides to create a burger patty with the guacamole inside, shaping it the best you can. It's okay if guacamole seeps out of the edges a bit.
7. Repeat with the rest so you have 4 burger patties. If you don't use all of the guacamole, serve it as a topping with the cooked burgers.
8. Grease and heat the grill or a grill pan over medium high heat.
9. Cook the burgers for 4 minutes on each side, until cooked through.
10. Serve with your favorite toppings!

Calories 374 Calories from Fat 270, Total Fat 30g 46%, Saturated Fat 10g 50%, Cholesterol 81mg 27%, Sodium 516mg 22%, Potassium 550mg 16%, Total Carbohydrates 6g 2%, Dietary Fiber 3g 12%, Sugars 1g, Protein 21g 42%, Vitamin A 1.7%, Vitamin C 9.4%, Calcium 2.9%, Iron 14.7%

Instant Pot Chicken and Mushrooms

Prep Time: 5 mins || Cook Time: 30 mins

Yield: 6 servings

Ingredients

- tablespoons avocado oil
- 1 large onion, diced
- cloves garlic, minced
- 1 bay leaf
- 2 cups sliced baby bella or cremini mushrooms
- 2 sprigs rosemary
- 2 pounds boneless skinless chicken thighs
- 2 teaspoons fine salt
- 1 teaspoon garlic powder
- 1 tsp ginger
- ½ teaspoon mace
- 2 tablespoons red wine vinegar
- ½ cup additive free coconut cream (water and coconut only)

Instructions

1. Heat your pressure cooker on sauce mode.
2. Add in the avocado oil, onion, garlic and bay leaf. Sauté for 8-10 minutes until tender. Add in the mushrooms and rosemary. Sauté for another 5 minutes until browned and tender.
3. Add in the chicken thighs and seasoning. Sauté, stirring occasionally until the chicken is mostly browned. Then add in the vinegar and stir, scrapping up any seasoning that stuck to the bottom of the pan.
4. Add in ¼ cup of cream. Cancel the sauté function, close the lid and set to pressure cook on high for 10 minutes.
5. When it's done, release the pressure manually. Open the lid and set to reduce or sauté until it comes to a simmer.
6. Stir, shredding the chicken with tongs or forks. Reduce the liquid by half, then stir in the remaining cream until smooth.
7. Transfer the chicken and sauce to a serving bowl. Let it cool for 5-10 minutes before serving, the sauce will get extra creamy in this time.

Serving Size: 6, Calories: 263, Fat: 15, Carbohydrates: 2, Fiber: 0, Protein: 30

Avocado Stuffed Meatballs!

Cook Time: 25 mins || Prep Time: 10 mins

Serves: 10 meatballs

Filled with creamy avocado, these keto chicken meatballs are about to become your new favorite snack.

Ingredients

- 1 lb ground pasture-raised chicken breast
- 1/4 t garlic powder
- T parsley, finely chopped
- 1/2 t sea salt
- 1 ripe avocado, mashed until smooth
- 1 T avocado oil

Instructions

1. In a large mixing bowl, combine chicken, garlic powder, parsley and sea salt. Mix until combined.
2. Form the mixture into 10 golf ball-sized meatballs, reserving about a half a cup of the meat. Create a divot in the center of each meatball and fill with ½ teaspoon of mashed avocado. Cover divot with 1 tablespoon from the reserved ground chicken to seal.
3. Heat oil over medium heat in a skillet. Add 4-5 meatballs and cook 12 minutes, turning meatballs to evenly brown on all sides. Set aside and keep warm.
4. Repeat with remaining meatballs, and serve!

Total fat: 5.5g | Net carbs: 0.5 | Protein: 11g

Keto & Whole30 Egg Salad

Serves: 8

Prep Time: 5 mins ||

Course: Breakfast

This keto and Whole30 egg salad is healthy and so easy to make. It's a classic recipe with an addicting crunch from the delicious bacon.

Ingredients

- hard boiled eggs*
- 1/4 cup red onion diced
- 8 slices sugar free bacon cooked and crumbled
- 3/4 cup paleo mayonnaise or more to taste
- 1 tbsp dijon mustard
- 2 tbsp fresh chives thinly sliced
- 1/2 tsp sea salt or more to taste
- 1/4 tsp ground black pepper
- 1/4 tsp smoked paprika

Instructions

1   Peel the eggs and chop into small pieces. Place in a large bowl.
2   Add the rest of the ingredients to the bowl.
3   Use a spoon to stir together until combined.
4   Taste to adjust creaminess and seasoning with more mayo or salt.
5   Refrigerate for at least 2 hours before serving.

Calories 332 Calories from Fat 270

Total Fat 30g 46%, Saturated Fat 7g 35%, Cholesterol 268mg 89%, Sodium 539mg 22%, Potassium 141mg 4%, Total Carbohydrates 1g 0%, Protein 11g 22%, Vitamin A 8.8%, Vitamin C 1%, Calcium 3.9%, Iron 7.3%

*My favorite method for hard boiling eggs is in the Instant Pot.

- Pour 1 cup of water in, place a steamer rack in the pot, and add the eggs.
- Cook on manual pressure on High for 5 minutes. Let it release naturally pressure for 5 minutes. Place in an ice bath for at least 5 minutes, before peeling.

Easy Hard Boiled Eggs

Ever since I got the Instant Pot, it's the only thing I use to make hard boiled eggs because it's easy, quick, and they come out perfect and easy-to-peel every time. Don't have one? No worries. Here are both stove top and Instant Pot methods to make hard boiled eggs for this Whole30 egg salad:

Stove Top Method

1. Bring water to a boil in a saucepan.
2. Take out eggs straight from the fridge, then lower the eggs into the water so they don't break, and let it come to a boil again. Once it does, lower the heat, and let the eggs simmer for 11 minutes.
3. Prepare a large bowl with an ice bath.
4. Once the eggs are done cooking, place them in the ice bath for at least 15 minutes.
5. Peel the eggs under cold running water.

Instant Pot Method

1. Pour 1 cup of water into the Instant Pot, and place a steamer basket or the trivet it came with over the water.
2. Place the eggs on the steamer basket or the trivet.
3. Close the lid, and make the sure the pressure valve is set to Sealing.
4. Cook on high on Manual for 5 minutes, and prepare an ice bath.
5. Once it beeps to a finish, naturally depressurize for 5 minutes, then release the pressure.
6. Immediately transfer the eggs to the ice bath and let it sit for at least 5 minutes.
7. Peel the eggs. They should be peel easily!

Southwest Salmon Cakes with Avocado Ranch Aioli

Prep Time: 5 Mins // Cook Time: 25 Mins

Yield: 8

Recipe Type: Breakfast

A simple salmon cake recipe with a southwest twist and the yummiest aioli sauce for dipping!

Ingredients

- Salmon Cakes
- 4 6 oz cans boneless/skinless salmon, drained I like Wild Planet brand!
- 1/2 medium red onion diced
- 1/8 cup chopped fresh cilantro can use parsley if you prefer!
- 1 tbsp coconut aminos
- 1 tbsp dijon mustard
- 1/2 cup mayo
- 2 eggs
- 1/3 cup almond flour
- 1 tsp sea salt
- 1 tsp cumin
- 1 tsp chili powder
- 1 tsp garlic powder
- 1/2 tsp paprika

- 1 tbsp ghee or olive oil

Avocado Ranch Aioli

- 1 large avocado peeled and pitted
- 1/3 cup mayo
- 1 tbsp fresh lemon juice
- 2 cloves minced garlic
- 1/4 tsp sea salt
- 1/2 tsp dried parsley
- 1/2 tsp dried minced onion
- 1/2 tsp dried dill
- 1/2 tsp dried chives
- 2 tbsp water more if you want it thinner

Instructions

1. Preheat oven to 425. Combine all salmon cake ingredients in a large bowl and mix well, making sure to break up all of the salmon pieces.
2. Line a baking sheet with parchment paper. Use a pastry brush to spread cooking oil of choice over the parchment paper.
3. Use a 1/3 cup measuring cup to scoop up the mixture and form 8 1-inch thick patties using your hands. Place them on the baking sheet.
4. Bake for 15 mins, then remove from the oven and flip using a spatula. Return them to the oven for an additional 10 minutes until browned and cooked through.
5. While the cakes are baking, make the aioli. Combine all aioli ingredients in a blender and blend on high for 30 seconds. Add water as needed until desired consistency is reached.
6. Serve the salmon cakes with the aioli. Enjoy!

Paleo Breakfast Fried Rice

Prep Time: 5 Mins // Cook Time: 15 Mins

Yield: 4

Recipe Type: Breakfast

This paleo breakfast fried rice is the best of both worlds: breakfast & Chinese food! Low carb cauliflower fried rice is combined with bacon and eggs to make the ultimate breakfast the entire family will love.

Ingredients

- 2 tbsp sesame oil
- 1 16 oz package frozen cauliflower rice
- 8 pieces sugar free bacon
- 3 eggs beaten **(Omit for AIP)**
- 1/2 medium onion diced
- 1/2 cup diced carrots
- 3 cloves garlic minced
- 1/2 tsp sea salt more to taste
- 1/4 cup coconut aminos
- 3 green onions diced for garnish

Instructions

1. Cook bacon using my easy baked method (or method of choice!). Meanwhile, heat a large non-stick skillet over medium high heat.
2. Add sesame oil. Once hot, add the onion, carrots, and garlic. Sauté for 3-4 minutes until onion and carrots begin to soften. Add in the frozen cauliflower rice. Cook for an additional 3-4 minutes.
3. Add in the sea salt and coconut aminos and stir to combine. Push the mixture over to one side of the pan to make some room for scrambling your eggs.
4. Pour the beaten eggs into the pan and stir until cooked through, then toss them with the rest of the fried rice.
5. When the bacon is done, drain it on a paper towel and break it into 1 inch pieces. Add to the cauliflower rice and stir to combine. Serve topped with green onions and enjoy!

SIDE DISH

Paleo Creamed Spinach with Bacon

Prep Time: 5 minutes || Cook Time: 20 minutes

Servings: 4 servings

Calories: 214kcal

Course: Side Dish

This comforting paleo creamed spinach with bacon uses pureed cauliflower for that rich, creamy texture. You'll never know that it's way healthier when you taste how amazingly addicting it is!

Ingredients

- 4 slices bacon
- 2 cups cauliflower florets
- 1/2 cup full fat coconut milk
- 1/3 cup bone broth or chicken broth or water
- 2 tsp apple cider vinegar
- 2 tsp dijon mustard
- 16 oz spinach fresh or frozen, roughly chopped
- 1 shallot chopped
- 4 cloves garlic minced
- 1/4 tsp sea salt or more to taste
- 1/4 tsp ground black pepper

Instructions

1   If using frozen spinach, defrost it first and squeeze out the liquid.
2   Heat a large skillet over medium heat and cook the bacon until crisp, about 6-7 minutes.

3   Remove from the pan and crumble when cool enough to handle.
4   Remove all but 1 tbsp of bacon fat in the pan and reserve the rest to use later in the recipe.
5   Add cauliflower florets to the pan and cook for 2 minutes.
6   Add broth and coconut milk to the pan, cover, and let everything come to a boil.
7   Lower the heat to simmer for 4-5 minutes until the cauliflower is tender.
8   Transfer the contents to a blender. Add apple cider vinegar and dijon mustard and blend until smooth. Set aside.
9   Heat a tablespoon of reserved bacon fat in a skillet over medium heat.
10 Add shallot and garlic, and cook stirring for 3-4 minutes until softened.
11 Add spinach, salt, and pepper, and toss until wilted and heated through.
12 Stir in cauliflower cream sauce and let everything heat through for 1 minute. Remove from heat.
13 Top with bacon bits or stir them in. Add more salt, if needed, before serving.

Amount Per Serving (1 serving – makes 4)

Calories 214Calories from Fat 153, Fat 17g26%, Saturated Fat 9g56%, Cholesterol 15mg5%, Sodium 437mg19%, Potassium 938mg27%, Carbohydrates 11g4%, Fiber 5g21%, Sugar 3g3%, Protein 9g18%, Vitamin A 10633IU213%, Vitamin C 58mg70%, Calcium 133mg13%, Iron 4mg22%

FOR AIP: Ensure bacon is compliant, use additive free coconut milk (water and coconut only as ingredients), omit dijon mustard, and black pepper

TIP: This might make a really good savory dip!

Cauliflower Tabouli (Tabbouleh) Salad

Prep Time: 10 minutes || Cook Time: 0 minutes

Yield: 2 servings

Category: Side Dish

Ingredients

- 100 g (3.5 oz) cauliflower florets
- a2 Tablespoons parsley, finely diced
- a3 mint leaves, finely diced
- a2 cherry tomatoes, diced (use 1/2 a small beet diced for AIP)
- 1 slice lemon diced
- 1 Tablespoon olive oil
- Salt and pepper to taste (omit pepper for AIP)

Instructions

1 Food process the cauliflower florets to form a couscous like texture. Make sure the florets and the food processor is dry to prevent a mash from forming instead.
2 Mix the food processed cauliflower florets with the finely diced herbs, tomatoes, lemon slice, olive oil, and salt and pepper to taste.

Serving Size: 90 g Calories: 80 Sugar: 2 g Fat: 7 g Carbohydrates: 5 g Fiber: 2 g Protein: 1 g

FOR AIP: use beet in place of tomatoes or use your imagination and try another AIP compliant veggie of your choice, omit pepper unless you've reintroduced

Keto Tuna Salad Recipe

Prep: 15 min

Serves: 2

Ingredients

- 1 cup cooked tuna, flaked
- 1 celery stalk, minced
- 1/2 cucumber, peeled and diced
- 1/2 bell pepper, diced
- 1/2 cup cherry tomatoes, diced
- 1 green onion, sliced
- 1/4 cup homemade mayonnaise
- 1 tbsp. fresh lemon juice
- 1 tbsp. Dijon mustard
- Sea salt and freshly ground black pepper

Instructions

1. In a bowl combine the Paleo mayonnaise, lemon juice, Dijon, and season to taste.
2. In another bowl combine all the other remaining ingredients.
3. Pour the mayo mixture over the tuna and toss until everything is well mixed.
4. Cover and refrigerate until ready to eat.
5. Serve the tuna salad over fresh greens.

FOR AIP: OMIT bell peppers and cherry tomatoes, use an AIP home-made mayo, omit Dijon Mustard and Black Pepper unless you've successfully reintroduced

Protein: 33g / 37%, Carbs: 7g / 8%, Fat: 22g / 55%

Roasted Broccoli & Cauliflower with Lemon & Garlic

Prep Time: 5 Mins || Cook Time: 35 Mins

Yield: 4-6

Recipe Type: side, Salad

Roasted vegetables are a healthy, easy side dish that can be added to any meal. This vegan-friendly broccoli and cauliflower dish uses just a few simple ingredients but is jam-packed with flavor.

Ingredients

- 1 head of broccoli
- 1/2 head of cauliflower
- 4 garlic cloves
- 1 lemon
- 2 tablespoons olive oil extra virgin
- salt and pepper to taste

Instructions

1. Preheat oven to 425 degrees.
2. Cut broccoli and cauliflower into large florets. Peel and thinly slice garlic cloves. Cut lemon in half and then into thin slices.
3. On a parchment paper-lined baking sheet toss broccoli, cauliflower, garlic cloves and lemon together with extra virgin olive oil. Coat evenly. Season generously with salt and pepper.
4. Roast in preheated oven for 35 minutes or until the floret edges begin to brown and curl.

Remove from the oven and give everything another good toss before serving. Enjoy!

Avocado Cauliflower Rice

Serves: 6 cups

Prep Time: 5 mins || Cook Time: 15 mins

Cooking Type: Baking

Course: Side dish

An easy side dish, this Avocado Cauliflower Rice takes riced cauliflower and adds smashed avocado, jalapeño, lime juice, and cilantro for a delicious paleo, Whole food, and low carb dish perfect to pair with just about anything!

Ingredients

- 6 cups cauliflower rice
- 1 tablespoon cooking fat (avocado oil, coconut oil)
- 1 cup diced yellow onion (120 grams)
- 3 cloves garlic, minced
- 2 large avocados, diced (300 grams)
- 1 jalapeño, diced
- 2 1/2 tablespoons lime juice
- 1/2 cup packed cilantro, roughly chopped
- salt and pepper, to taste

Instructions

1. Heat a large sauté pan over medium heat. Add oil and let it get hot. Once hot, add diced onions and sauté for 5 minutes until translucent, stirring occasionally. Add garlic and cook for another minute. Add the cauliflower rice and let cook for 6-7 minutes, stirring occasionally, until softened.
2. While the rice cooks, make the avocado mash. Add avocados, diced jalapeno, lime juice, and salt and pepper to a large bowl and mash with a fork until combined, but a little texture remains.
3. Once cauliflower rice is cooked to your preference, remove from heat. Add avocado mixture to cauliflower rice and mix well to combine. Stir in cilantro. Top more cilantro and jalapeño if desired. Enjoy!

Calories 151 Calories from Fat 90

Total Fat 10g 15%, Saturated Fat 2.6g 13%, Polyunsaturated Fat 0.1g, Monounsaturated Fat 5g, Potassium 715.9mg 20%, Carbohydrates 14g 5%, Dietary Fiber 7.4g 30%, Sugars 5.4g, Protein 4g 8%, Vitamin A 4.6%, Vitamin C 121.9%, Calcium 4.9%, Iron 5.7%

Guacamole Chicken Salad

Serves:3

Prep Time: 10 mins || Cook Time: 20 min

Cooking Type: Baking

Course: Side dish

Since guacamole and chicken salad are two of our favorite things, I decided it was time to combine them! This guacamole chicken salad is mayo-free, packed with flavor, protein, and perfect for easy lunches!

Ingredients

- 2 avocados medium
- 1/3 cup onion minced
- 2 cloves garlic minced
- 1-2 jalapeno pepper minced (adjust for spice preference)
- 2-3 Tbsp fresh lime juice or to taste
- 2 Tbsp chopped fresh cilantro plus more for garnish
- Sea salt to taste
- 1 lb chicken breast seasoned with salt and pepper and cooked (about 2-2.5 cups cooked) see below instructions for my cooking method

Instructions

Cook chicken (this step should be done ahead of time so the chicken has time to cool.)

1. Preheat your oven to 400 degrees and line a baking sheet with foil. Drizzle olive oil over chicken and turn to coat.
2. Season on both sides with sea salt, black pepper, plus onion + garlic powder, if desired. Bake in the preheated oven for 20 minutes or until cooked through (no longer pink in the middle and juices run clear.)
3. Allow chicken to cool completely, then either dice or shred depending on what you prefer for chicken salad.

assemble salad:

1. In a large bowl, add the cooked diced chicken with all remaining ingredients except for the salt. Mix well, mashing avocado as you mix.
2. Once fully combined, add sea salt to taste. Serve immediately, leftovers will keep for about a day in the refrigerator but because the avocado will brown, it won't last much longer than that. Enjoy!

Calories: 240kcalFat: 14gSaturated fat: 2gCholesterol: 58mgSodium: 111mgPotassium: 741mgCarbohydrates: 8gFiber: 5gSugar: 1gProtein: 21gVitamin A: 175%Vitamin C: 15.4%Calcium: 19%Iron: 0.8%

Roasted Garlic on the Grill

Serves: 20 cloves

Prep Time: 2 mins || Cook Time: 30 mins

Cooking Type: Baking

Course: Side dish

You won't believe how easy this is. With just 3 essential ingredients you have a creamy garlic spread.

Ingredients

- 2 garlic heads
- 2 teaspoons olive oil
- sea salt to taste

Instructions

1. Set up the grill for indirect heat and preheat to 350 - 400 degrees (or preheat oven).
2. Cut the top off of garlic heads, making sure each individual clove has the tip cut off so you can squeeze the garlic out easily once it's roasted.
3. Drizzle with olive oil, sprinkle with sea salt and wrap each garlic head in a double layer of foil.
4. Roast 30 - 45 minutes in a closed grill (or oven), until garlic feels soft when squeezed.

Note: one head of garlic contains about 10 cloves

Calories: 3kcal | Vitamin C: 0.1mg | Calcium: 1mg

Baked Asparagus

Prep Time: 15 Mins // **Cook Time:** 35 Mins

Servings: 6

Recipe Type: side

These are delicious just the way they are. Very healthy and healing for your gut. Asparagus has allot of health benefits and one main it's high in Fiber, High in Vitamins, Nourishes the digestive track and more!

Ingredients:

- 1-2 Bunches Organic Asparagus
- 5-8 Cloves Garlic
- 1 Tsp. Pink Salt
- 1 Tsp. Black Pepper
- 1 Tsp. paprika
- 1 Tbl Oregano
- 1 Tsp. Onion Powder
- 1 Tsp. Lemon or Lime Zest
- 2 Tbl Avocado Oil or Olive Oil Pure.
- Lemon or Lime Juice

Instructions:

1. Cut off 1 inch of the bottom root of the Asparagus and give it a good wash.
2. Place the Asparagus in the oven Pan, spread out.
3. In a little "Ceramic Mash bowl" place the Garlic with the spices and give it a good "Mash".
4. Add the wet ingredients to the mashed garlic, give it a good stir.
5. Pour onto the Asparagus.
6. Drizzle some Lemon or Lime juice (Which ever you prefer).
7. Bake on 350F for about 20-30 minutes. Don't over Bake (Don't let it discolor) Let there be a crisp to the Asparagus.
8. Enjoy!

Almond Ramp Pesto

Prep Time: 10 Mins // Cook Time: 45 Mins

Servings: 15

Calories: 137kcal

Ingredients

- 6 oz. Ramps
- 3/4 cup Olive Oil
- 1/2 cup Roasted almonds
- 1/4 cup Grated Parmesan Cheese
- 1 tsp. Crushed Chili Flakes
- 2 tsp. Red Wine Vinegar
- Salt & Pepper to taste **(Omit For AIP)**

Instructions

1. Once Ramp leaves are washed and patted dry rough chop the leaves into ribbons before adding to a food processor along with all other ingredients
2. Pulse food processor a few times before then continue to process for 10-15 seconds until the pesto reaches the consistency you prefer.
3. Taste for seasoning, then using a spatula scrape down the sides and pulse a few more times to fully combine
4. Scoop the pesto into small sandwich ziplock bags and press out as much air as possible before sealing the bag completely.
5. Store fresh for up to 2 weeks or freeze up to one year.

Calories: 137kcal | Carbohydrates: 2g | Protein: 1g | Fat: 13g | Saturated Fat: 1g| Cholesterol: 1mg | Sodium: 27mg | Potassium: 36mg | Vitamin A: 4.9% | Vitamin C: 1.6% | Calcium: 3.8% | Iron: 2.8%

Instant Pot Beef and Broccoli Soup

Prep Time: 10 Mins // Cook Time: 20 Mins

Servings: 2

Yield: 3 servings

Serving Size: 1/3 recipe

Your favorite takes out fake out made into a healthy soup!

Ingredients

- 1 pound steak tips
- 1 teaspoon baking powder
- 1 tablespoon coconut aminos
- 1 tablespoon Red Boat Fish Sauce
- 2 tablespoons ghee or coconut oil for AIP
- 3 cloves garlic, minced
- 2 teaspoons ground ginger
- 1 teaspoon fine salt
- 2 cups broccoli florets (1–2 crowns cut)
- 1 1/2 cup bone broth
- 2 tablespoon cashew butter or coconut cream for AIP

Instructions

1. Heat pressure cooker on sauté mode. While it heats toss the beef with the baking powder, let it sit for 2 minutes then add in the coconut aminos and fish sauce and toss to combine.
2. When the pot comes to temperature add in the ghee. The place the chunks of beef in the ghee, reserving the marinade. Sear for 3 minutes each side. Add in the marinade. Add in the garlic, ginger, salt and broccoli and stir well.
3. Add in the bone broth and stir well to deglaze the pot. Cancel the sauté function. Seal the lid and set to pressure cook on high for 15 minutes, when it's done cooking release the pressure manually.
4. Open the lid and use a slotted spoon or tongs to remove the beef chunks from the soup, set aside. Add in the cashew cream and use an immersion blender to blend the broccoli mix until smooth.
5. Add the beef chunks back in and stir. Serve hot!cTop with a fried egg, sesame oil or sesame seeds, green onions or enjoy as is!

CALORIES: 345.9, FAT: 17.7g, CARBOHYDRATES: 8.1g, FIBER: 2.3g, PROTEIN: 40.6g

MAIN DISH

Instant Pot Hard Boiled Eggs

Serves: 12

Prep Time: 1 mins || **Cook Time:** 5 min

Cooking Type: Instant Pot

Course: Main dish

The easiest way to make perfect hard boiled eggs - in the Instant Pot!

Ingredients

- 1 cup water
- large eggs

Instructions

1. Place steamer rack or trivet in the cooking pot. Add water and place eggs on the rack.
2. Set the program to Egg. Set time to 5 minutes and set pressure to low. Press start.
3. When cooking is done, press button to quick release pressure.
4. Remove eggs from pot and place in ice water bath to cool.

Calories: 62kcal | Carbohydrates: 0g | Protein: 5g | Fat: 4g | Saturated Fat: 1g | Cholesterol: 163mg | Sodium: 63mg | Potassium: 60mg | Sugar: 0g | Vitamin A: 240IU | Calcium: 25mg | Iron: 0.8mg

Rosemary & Garlic Whole30 Roast Beef

Course: Main Course

Prep Time: 5 minutes||Cook Time: 1 hour

Servings: 6 servings

Calories: 317kcal

This Rosemary & Garlic Whole30 Roast Beef is a fancy but easy holiday main dish, and the leftovers are just as amazing as when it's fresh out of the oven!

Ingredients

- 3 lb beef top round roast* or eye of round roast or bottom round roast
- 1 tbsp extra virgin olive oil
- 4 garlic cloves minced
- 1 tbsp chopped fresh rosemary
- 1 tsp sea salt
- 1/2 tsp ground black pepper omit for AIP

Instructions

1. Remove the beef from the fridge 45 minutes before cooking to let it come to a a room temperature. This will ensure even cooking.
2. Preheat the oven to 375 degrees F.
3. Use a twine to tie the meat at 2 inch intervals.
4. Combine the olive oil and the rest of the ingredients in a bowl so a thick paste forms, and coat the meat with this mixture.
5. Place on a roasting rack over a pan and roast in the oven for about 1 hour, or until a thermometer inserted into the center reads 130 degrees for medium rare.
6. Remove from the oven, tent with a foil, and let it rest for 15-20 minutes. The temperature will rise about 5 degrees.

7   Slice thinly and enjoy!

Amount Per Serving (1 serving)

Calories 317Calories from Fat 90, Fat 10g15%, Saturated Fat 3g19%, Cholesterol 138mg46%, Sodium 533mg23%, Potassium 854mg24%, Carbohydrates 1g0%, Fiber 1g4%, Sugar 1g1%, Protein 53g106%, Vitamin A 19IU0%Vitamin C 1mg1%, Calcium 56mg6%, 5mg28%

Notes

*If using a different sized roast, adjust the cooking time to 20 minutes per pound

Loaded Chicken Taco Dip

Serves: 12

Prep Time: 25 mins ||

Cooking Type: Mashing

Course: Appetizer

This loaded chicken taco dip is full of all your favorites! An easy homemade guacamole, taco seasoned chicken, chipotle ranch sauce, salsa, shredded veggies and jalapeno peppers. Serve with fresh cut veggies for a fun appetizer or meal. Keto, Whole30, and Paleo.

Ingredients

chicken:

- 2 cups chicken breasts cooked and shredded
- 1/4 cup avocado oil or light olive oil
- 1/2 tsp sea salt
- Juice of 2 small limes about 1 1/2 tbsp
- 2 tsp chili powder
- 1/2 tsp onion powder
- 1/2 tsp garlic powder
- 1/4 tsp chipotle powder
- 1/2 tsp cumin

guacamole:

- 2 avocados
- 1/4 cup onion minced
- 2 clove garlic minced
- 1 med jalapeno pepper minced
- 2 Tbsp fresh lime juice or to taste
- 2 Tbsp chopped fresh cilantro plus more for garnish
- Sea salt to taste

chipotle ranch:

- 1 cup homemade mayo
- 2 tsp fresh lime juice or lemon juice
- 1 tsp onion powder
- 1 tsp garlic powder
- 2 tsp dried chives
- 1/2 tsp chipotle powder
- 1/2 tsp paprika

additional ingredients:

- 1/2 cup salsa compliant
- 1/3 cup Shredded Brussels Sprouts Or lettuce, or cabbage
- 2-3 Jalapeño peppers thinly sliced
- Additional cilantro for garnish, if desired

Instructions

1 To prepare the chicken, whisk together the oil, salt, line juice and spices in a bowl until fully combined, then toss with the shredded chicken.
2 Prepare guacamole by mashing all ingredients together. For the chipotle ranch, whisk together all ingredients in a small bowl.
3 Assemble the dip: In an 8 x 8 dish (or comparably sized dish/container) layer the guac, chicken, chipotle ranch, salsa, shredded Brussels sprouts, jalapeno, and any additional cilantro.
4 Serve immediately with fresh cut veggies, sweet potato fries or tostones. Store leftovers in an airtight container in the refrigerator for up to 3 days. Enjoy!

Calories: 262kcalFat: 24gSaturated fat: 3gCholesterol: 23mgSodium: 334mgPotassium: 336mgCarbohydrates: 5gFiber: 3gSugar: 1gProtein: 6gVitamin A: 935%Vitamin C: 13.2%Calcium: 19%Iron: 0.7%

Immune Boosting Vegetable Soup

(Makes 4 bowls)

Ingredients:

- 1/2 head cabbage, chopped (can be green, red, or mixed)
- 1 cup celery, diced
- 1 cup yellow onion, diced
- q3 cloves garlic, minced
- 1/2 cup rainbow carrots, diced
- 1 cup kale, chopped
- q4 cups organic bone broth
- 1 teaspoon oregano
- 1 teaspoon basil
- 1 teaspoon turmeric
- salt and pepper to taste

Instructions

1) In a large saucepan or dutch oven, melt 2 tablespoons grass-fed butter or ghee over a medium heat.
2) Add celery, onions, and carrots. Saute until lightly tender.
3) Stir in garlic and seasonings.
4) Add bone broth, cabbage, and kale.
5) Bring to a boil and then reduce heat. Simmer for 30 minutes on low, or until ready to eat.
6) Enjoy! Store in the fridge. This soup will last 3-5 days.

FOR AIP: Omit pepper unless you've reintroduced

Creamy Avocado Keto Chicken Salad

Prep Time: 15 minutes

Total Time: 15 minutes

Yield: 4

Serving Size: 1

Ingredients

- 2 cups cooked chicken, finely diced
- 1/3 cup mayo
- 1 medium avocado, peeled, halved and pitted
- 1 stalk celery, finely diced
- 2 tbsp minced red onion
- 2 tbsp cilantro, finely chopped
- 1 tbsp fresh lemon juice
- salt and pepper to taste

Instructions

1. In food processor place the mayo, half of avocado, lemon juice, salt and black pepper to taste and process until smooth.
2. Cut the remaining avocado into small cubes.
3. In a bowl place the chicken, avocado, celery, red onion and cilantro.
4. Add the mayo mixture and mix to combine.
5. Serve with toasted keto bread or tortillas.

Calories: 172, Carbohydrates: 1.3 g, Fat: 17.6 g, Sugar: 0.5 g, Protein: 2.2 g

FOR AIP: use an AIP Mayo and omit pepper unless you've reintroduced

Easy Paleo Salmon Bowls

Makes: 4 bowls

Ingredients:

For the salmon:

- 4 salmon fillets
- 1 tsp smoked paprika
- 1 tsp garlic powder
- 1/4 tsp each of salt and pepper

For the avocado crema:

- 1 ripe organic avocado
- 1/3 cup full fat coconut milk
- 1/4 cup fresh cilantro minced
- 1 tablespoon fresh lime juice, lime zest
- 1 teaspoon garlic powder
- 1 teaspoon onion powder

For the rest of the bowl:

- 8 cups dark leafy greens, organic

- 2 cups roasted vegetables of choice (zucchini and squash are my faves)
- additional seasoning of choice

Instructions

1) Preheat oven to 400° Fahrenheit. Place chopped vegetables on the baking sheet and drizzle with extra virgin olive oil. Place in the oven to bake for 40 minutes, or until cooked through.
2) When the vegetables are half way done, place salmon fillets on a lined baking sheet and season with the smoked paprika, garlic powder and a pinch each of salt and pepper. Place in the oven to bake for 15-20 until flaky with a fork. Cooking time will vary depending on the size of your fillets.
3) While the salmon and vegetables are cooking, make your avocado crema. Add avocado, coconut milk, cilantro, lime juice, garlic powder, onion powder, salt and pepper to taste in a blender or food processor and pulse until sauce is creamy.
4) Divide leafy greens between four bowls and add a tablespoon of sauce to each. Massage sauce into the greens.
5) Remove vegetables and salmon from the oven. Let cool slightly for 2-3 minutes.
6) Add vegetables to the bowls and top them with a salmon fillet. Generously drizzle avocado sauce over the top of the salmon, season and enjoy!

FOR AIP: Omit paprika and pepper, use additive free coconut milk (water and coconut only)

Chicken and Pesto Spaghetti Squash Boats

Serves: 2

Ingredients:

- 1 medium organic spaghetti squash
- 2 tablespoons grass-fed butter or cooking oil
- 3/4 lb. organic chicken breasts
- 1 medium yellow onion, diced
- 1/2 teaspoon salt
- 1/2 teaspoon pepper
- 1/2 cup pesto (look for dairy-free brands or make your own)
- 2 teaspoons nutritional yeast or grass-fed, raw cheese

Instructions

1. Preheat your oven to 350F. Place the entire spaghetti squash on a rimmed baking sheet for 1 hour, turning the squash half way through. Allow to cool for 20 minutes (or longer) until cool enough to handle.
2. While the spaghetti squash is cooling, heat a large skillet over medium high heat. Add the cooking oil, onion, chicken, salt and pepper. Cook for 10-15 minutes until the onions are soft and the chicken is cooked through.
3. Using a large knife, cut the spaghetti squash in half. Use a spoon to scoop out the seeds, and throw away. Use a fork to shred the spaghetti squash into a large bowl.

4   Add in the cooked chicken and onion mix, and pesto sauce. Toss to combine.
5   Add to the empty spaghetti squash skin and top with nutritional yeast or raw cheese. We love ours with a side salad for extra greens and nutrients!

FOR AIP: use avocado oil, olive oil or coconut oil NOT butter, omit pepper unless you've reintroduced and use a home-made AIP pesto, use NON-fortified nutritional yeast.

Addictive Roasted Broccoli and Mushrooms with Onion Wedges

Serving Size: 1

Servings/Recipe: 4

Calories: 186

Ingredients

- 1 large head broccoli, cut into florets
- ½ pound mushrooms, quartered
- j2 small red onions, cut into wedges
- j3 tbsp olive oil
- 1 tbsp balsamic vinegar or more to taste
- salt and ground black pepper to taste

Instructions

1. Preheat oven to 425°F.
2. Place the broccoli florets, mushrooms and red onion on a large baking sheet.
3. Drizzle with olive oil and toss to coat.
4. Season to taste with salt and black pepper.
5. Roast in preheat oven for 20-25 minutes or until lightly brown and tender.
6. Remove from the oven.
7. Drizzle with balsamic vinegar and toss to coat.
8. Serve immediately.

Carbohydrates: 19 g, Fat: 11.1 g, Sugar: 6.5 g, Protein: 7.6 g, Fiber: 6.3 g, Calories: 186 kcal, Potassium: 848.3 mg, Vitamin A: 59.2 µg, Vitamin C: 173.3 mg, Folic Acid (B9): 136.2 µg, Sodium: 690 mg

FOR AIP: Omit black pepper unless you've reintroduced

Loaded Cauliflower Soup

This loaded cauliflower soup is a lighter, veggie-filled take on classic potato soup!

Prep Time: 15 minutes || Cook Time: 15 minutes

Total Time: 30 minutes

Yield: 6-8 servings

Category: Dinner

Ingredients

- 2 medium heads cauliflower
- 4 cups chicken broth*
- 1 cup sour cream (substitute full-fat coconut milk for dairy-free/Whole 30)
- 1 tablespoon lemon juice (about 1/2 lemon)
- 1/2 teaspoon garlic powder
- 1/2 teaspoon onion powder
- 1/2 teaspoon sea salt
- 6 slices cooked and crumbled bacon, for garnish
- 1 cup shredded cheddar cheese, for garnish (omit for dairy-free/Whole 30)
- Sliced green onions, for garnish

Instructions

Stovetop

1. Cut the cauliflower heads into florets, removing the tough inner core. Place the cauliflower florets and 3 cups of the broth in a large pot with matching lid over medium high heat.
2. Bring to a boil, then place the lid on the pot and reduce the heat to low to cook for 15 minutes, until the cauliflower is tender.
3. Remove the cauliflower from the pot and add to a high powered blender, like a Vitamix, and blend for 1-2 minutes until smooth.
4. Add the garlic powder, onion powder, salt, sour cream, and lemon juice, then blend again on high for an additional 30 seconds until fully combined. Pour in additional broth to your desired consistency.
5. Pour the soup into bowls and top each with bacon, cheese, and green onions. Enjoy!

Instant Pot

1. Add the cauliflower florets and broth to the Instant Pot, then place the lid on the pot, ensure it is sealed, and set to cook for 5 minutes.
2. Remove the cauliflower from the pot and add to a high powered blender, like a Vitamix, and blend for 1-2 minutes until smooth.

3   Add the garlic powder, onion powder, salt, sour cream, and lemon juice, then blend again on high for an additional 30 seconds until fully combined. Pour in additional broth to your desired consistency.

4   Pour the soup into bowls and top each with bacon, cheese, and green onions. Enjoy!

NOTES

*With 4 cups broth, this soup has a thicker, more mash-like texture. If you like a thinner soup, add 1-2 cups additional broth to your liking.

FOR AIP: use additive free coconut milk (water and coconut only) - not sour cream, ensure bacon is compliant (search the group for "baked bacon" if you need info on that), omit optional cheddar cheese garnish

Instant pot whole chicken

Prep Time: 10 Mins || Cook Time: 35 Mins

Yield: Serves 4-6

Method: Instant Pot

This Whole30 instant pot whole chicken is one of the easiest ways to get a healthy, paleo dinner on the table or meal prep done quickly.

With the lemon and spices, it's a full-of-flavor, juicy and uncomplicated paleo, keto or Whole30 chicken recipe. Plus, the options for the leftover chicken is endless

Ingredients

- 3–5 pound whole chicken, innards removed
- 1–2 tablespoons avocado oil for searing
- 1 tablespoon ghee
- Juice from 1 lemon
- 1 teaspoon garlic powder
- 1 and 1/2 teaspoon salt
- ½ teaspoon thyme
- 1 teaspoon chili powder
- ½ teaspoon pepper
- 1 white onion, quartered
- 1 cup chicken or vegetable broth

Instructions

1. In a small bowl, combine all of the spices with the lemon juice and ghee. Stir really well to create a paste.
2. Dry chicken thoroughly and then season chicken, ensuring to rub paste under the skin. Stuff cavity with onion quarters.
3. Set instant pot to the saute setting. Add oil and allow to heat up, and then add the whole chicken, breast side down, and sear, about 3-4 minutes. Using tongs, flip the chicken over and sear for an additional 3-4 minutes; remove chicken and set aside.
4. Insert the metal trivet into the instant pot and add the broth. Set the chicken on top of the trivet.
5. Set to manual high pressure for 25 minutes, and set to valve to sealing. When finished cooking, do a quick release. Allow to rest for a few minutes to lock in all of the juices.
6. Serve immediately with additional lemon slices or thyme.

FOR AIP: use coconut oil not ghee, omit chili powder and pepper

Shrimp Etouffee

Course: Lunch, Main Course

Servings: 4

A rich roux-based sauce boasting Cajun flavors compliments the umami of shrimp. Ladle over riced veggies of your choice, with a squeeze of fresh lemon and a dash of hot sauce to make this Southern classic complete.

Ingredients

- 3 Tb lard
- 1 small sweet onion diced
- 1 stalk celery diced
- 1/2 bell pepper diced (AIP: sub 1 more stalk celery or 1 small carrot)
- 1/4 cup cassava flour
- 2 large cloves garlic pressed
- 1 Tb Cajun seasoning (AIP: sub 1/2 tsp garlic powder, 1/2 tsp onion powder, 1/4 tsp Italian seasoning, 1 tsp ginger powder, 1 tsp horseradish powder, and 1/4 tsp Himalayan salt)
- 1 Tb dried parsley
- 1/2 tsp Himalayan salt
- 1 to 2 tsp Frank's Red Hot (AIP: sub 1 to 2 tsp lemon juice)
- 3 cups bone broth fish, chicken or pork
- 1 bay leaf
- 1 lb medium shrimp peeled, deveined, tails removed and strained very well (you can also use crawfish, cubed skinless fish or scallops)
- lemon wedges

Instructions

1. Press SAUTE. When display reads HOT, add the lard, onion, celery and bell pepper. Stir well.
2. Cook, stirring occasionally, for 7 minutes or until browned and slightly caramelized.
3. Press CANCEL, then vigorously stir in cassava flour until mixture bonds together. Stir in garlic, Cajun seasoning, parsley, salt and hot sauce.
4. Press SAUTE. Press ADJUST until LESS is illuminated.
5. Drizzle in 1 cup of the bone broth, stirring continuously to prevent lumps. When mixture is smooth, slowly add remaining 2 cups broth while stirring, then add bay leaf.
6. Bring to a simmer, stirring and scraping the bottom every couple of minutes to prevent sticking. Cook this way for 10 to 15 minutes, or until sauce is thickened and reduced to 2/3.
7. Stir in shrimp. Cook for 2 minutes, stirring continuously. Press CANCEL.
8. (Shrimp will continue to cook slightly in the hot gravy, so it is best to stop the heat underneath just before they look completely done.)
9. Serve in bowls with lemon wedges and a splash of hot sauce.

Notes

NOTES: If you tolerate ghee, substitute it for the lard and enjoy the traditional buttery flavor of the roux. Serve over your favorite riced veggies or a baked potato.

FOR AIP:

- Do NOT use bell pepper diced use 1 more stalk celery or 1 small carrot
- For the Cajun seasoning, use 1/2 tsp garlic powder, 1/2 tsp onion powder, 1/4 tsp Italian seasoning 1 tsp ginger powder, 1 tsp horseradish powder, and 1/4 tsp Himalayan salt
- Replace Hot Sauce with 1 to 2 tsp lemon juice, do NOT use ghee in place of lard as noted in optional substitutions at the end of the recipe

Pumpkin Spice Spatchcock Chicken

Course: Main Course

Prep Time: 15 Minutes || Cook Time: 1 Hour

Total Time: 1 Hour 15 Minutes

Servings: 6

Pumpkin spice, sweet orange & aromatic garlic with tender onions make for an addictive spatchcocked, crispy-skinned chicken with dippable jus. Whole30 and Keto with AIP option.

Ingredients

- 1 Tb Primal Palate Pumpkin Pie Spice for AIP use 1 & 1/2 tsp cinnamon, 1 tsp ginger powder, 1/4 tsp mace and 1/2 tsp clove.
- 1 tsp Himalayan salt
- 1/16 tsp cayenne pepper for AIP omit
- zest of 1/2 and all juice of 1 medium orange
- 1 Tb coconut aminos
- 1 Tb refined avocado oil
- 4 large cloves garlic pressed
- 2 Tb fresh parsley chopped
- 1 medium red onion sliced into 1/4" circles
- 6 lb whole chicken

Instructions

1. To make the marinade: In a small bowl, mix together the Pumpkin Pie Spice blend, salt and cayenne with a fork.
2. Vigorously stir in the orange zest and juice, aminos and oil, then stir in the garlic and parsley. Set aside.
3. Lay a piece of parchment down on a large sheet pan and lay the onion circles in an even layer in the center. Set aside.
4. Use sharp, heavy duty kitchen shears to completely remove the spine from the chicken, and trim off any excessive flaps of fatty skin. (Save trimmed-off parts for making bone broth if you like.)
5. Lay the chicken skin-side-up over the onions, and press down very firmly on the center of the chicken until you hear a couple of cracks. This helps to flatten the chicken for even cooking.
6. Stir the marinade once more, then drizzle it all over the top of the chicken. It's going to drip down over the edges but that's OK.
7. Use your hands to massage the marinade into the chicken skin on top, then pick up the chicken with one hand and massage the under part / flesh with the marinade that poured onto the pan.
8. Leave at room temperature for 1 hour to allow flavors to soak into the chicken. Letting the chicken rest at room temp also to helps the chicken cook more evenly later.

9 Set oven to 425 F, then bake chicken for 1 hour, basting halfway through. Chicken is done when the skin is crispy and a lovely browned color, and temperature taken from the thickest part of the chicken reads at least 165 F.

10 Rest for 20 minutes before carving to keep those precious juices inside the meat!

FOR AIP: Use the suggested replacement - not Pumpkin Pie Spice (it contains non-compliant ingredients), and omit cayenne pepper

Creamy Chicken Thighs with Bacon Brussels

Course: Main Course

Prep Time: 15 Minutes || Cook Time: 1 Hour

Serves: 6

Ingredients:

Sauce:

- 3 tablespoons grass-fed butter, Ghee, or coconut oil
- 1 yellow onion, chopped
- 3 cloves minced garlic
- 2 tablespoons arrowroot starch
- 1 1/2 cups bone broth
- 1/2 cup full fat coconut milk
- 1/2 Tbsp brown mustard
- 1 1/2 Tbsp nutritional yeast
- 1/4 teaspoon sea salt
- 1/8 teaspoon black pepper
- 1 teaspoon fresh rosemary
- 1 lb organic chicken thighs

- 3 cups shaved brussel sprouts
- 3 Tbsp grass-fed butter, Ghee, or coconut oil
- Sea salt and pepper
- 8 slices bacon (nitrate-free, organic)

Instructions

1. Preheat your oven to 425F.
2. In a cast iron skillet, melt 2 tablespoons grass-fed butter. Place chicken thighs in the skillet and sprinkle with salt and pepper. Cook for 6 minutes on each side, or until skin has crisped.
3. On a baking sheet, arrange your brussel sprouts and coat with olive oil and seasoning. Add chicken thighs to the baking sheet.
4. Roast chicken and brussel sprouts for 20-25 minutes.
5. While the chicken thighs and brussel sprouts roast, cook the bacon until crisp in a large skillet. Set aside.
6. For the sauce, use the bacon fat as the base. Add the onions to the skillet, cook until translucent and fragrant, then add the garlic and continue to cook until soft.
7. Whisk the arrowroot flour into the broth and add it to the skillet, then add the coconut milk, mustard and nutritional yeast, while whisking. Raise the heat and bring to a boil. Once boiling, lower to a simmer and continue to stir and cook for another minute, until thick.
8. Stir in salt and pepper to taste, add the fresh herbs, then remove from heat.
9. Add the roasted brussel sprouts and chicken to the skillet on top of the sauce mixture, lightly stir to evenly coat.
10. Add the chopped bacon to the skillet.
11. Pop back in the oven at 400F for an extra 10-15 minutes. Serve hot and enjoy!

FOR AIP: an all cases use coconut oil not ghee or butter, use additive free coconut milk (water and coconut only) omit brown mustard, use NON-Fortified nutritional yeast omit black pepper, ensure bacon is compliant

Grilled Greek Souvlaki Chicken Wings

Prep time: 1 hour || Cook time: 1 hour 15 mins

Serves: 4-6 servings

Ingredients

- 3-5 lbs organic chicken wings, cut into two pieces - drumstick and wing*

Marinade:

- ½ cup lemon juice
- w4 cloves garlic, minced
- 1 tablespoon dried oregano
- extra virgin olive oil
- salt and pepper

Finishing Sauce:

- ⅓ cup lemon juice
- ⅓ cup extra virgin olive oil
- 1½ teaspoons dried oregano
- ½ teaspoon salt
- black pepper, to taste
- crumbled sheep's milk feta cheese, optional

For Serving:

- lemon zest
- lemon wedges
- feta cheese crumbles
- fresh oregano or dill
- black olives
- tzatziki sauce

Instructions

1. Add the chicken wings to a shallow baking dish. Add the lemon juice, garlic, salt, pepper and give it all a stir and finish with the olive oil. Cover and refrigerate for at least 1 hour or up to overnight.
2. When ready to grill, remove the chicken wings from the fridge and using tongs remove the wings from the marinade and place on a baking sheet to take out to the grill.
3. Preheat your grill to hot. All the burners. Close the cover to allow to heat up.
4. Turn off center two burners (or 1, depending on grill). Leave outside burners set to hot. Place wings on the hot grill over center burners (that should be off) and/or on top shelf rack. Note the wings on the top rack will cook faster. Close the grill.

5   At no time should the wings ever be over direct heat/flame. We are indirect cooking them.
6   Check the wings at 15 minutes, just to be sure there are no wings too close to the direct flame, you can move around as needed if some get more heat, but don't flip yet. At this point the wings should still look somewhat pale, but not raw.
7   Check again at 30 minutes. At this point the top of the wings should have a nice, very light brown color. Flip all the wings over, the bottoms should be golden brown. Any wing that you can't pick up (stuck to the grill still) these may need another 5 minutes or so.
8   Check the wings at 45 minutes. Just to be sure nothing is getting too much heat. Swap any around as needed, if some are getting too much.
9   At 1 hour, have both a small and a medium sized bowl ready. Prepare the finishing sauce by adding all of the ingredients except the feta cheese, in a small mixing bowl. Whisk until well combined.
10 Remove the wings in groups of 4-8. Place into the medium bowl and pour in some of the finishing sauce (don't drown the wings). Crumble in a tablespoon or two of feta cheese. Shake the wings really well to coat.
11 Place the coated wings on the top rack. If your grill doesn't have a top rack, place back in the center of the grill where the burners are off. Continue with remaining wings and continue adding the sauce until all are sauced and added back to the grill.
12 If all the wings are on the top rack turn on all burners to high. (If not, leave off the burners where the wings are) close the cover and in increments of 3-5 minutes, check the wings you are cooking until desired crispness is achieved. Remove from the grill, garnish as you would like and serve.

For paleo, Whole30, AIP - leave out the feta cheese and make dairy-free tzatziki.
For AIP: leave out black pepper, if you choose to.

- I always recommend sourcing pasture-raised chicken, from a local farmer, if you can. Organic is next best.
- The amount of wings that you can cook at once will depend on your grill size, as you can't load up and crowd the grill with this cooking method. We find that 5lbs is the max on our standard sized-grill. This is with some wings on the top rack and some on the center of the grill.

For optional toppings: ensure olives are compliant (should be in a simple salt brine or packed in pure olive oil).

Chicken and Bacon Sausages Recipe

Prep Time: 10 minutes || **Cook Time:** 20 minutes

Yield: 12 servings

Category: Breakfast, Lunch

Ingredients

- 2 large chicken breasts, or use 1 lb ground chicken
- 2 slices bacon, cooked and broken into small bits
- 1 egg, whisked (omit for AIP)
- 2 Tablespoons Italian seasoning
- 2 teaspoons garlic powder
- 2 teaspoons onion powder
- Salt and pepper

Instructions

1 Preheat oven to 425 F (220 C).
2 Food process all the ingredients together.

3. Form 12 thin patties (1/2-inch thick) from the meat mixture and place on a baking tray lined with foil (so you don't need to wash the baking tray).
4. Bake for 20 minutes. Check with a meat thermometer that the internal temperature of a patty near the middle of the tray is 170 F (76 C).
5. Cool and store in fridge or freezer (reheat them easily in the mornings in the skillet or in the microwave).

(You can also pan-fry the raw sausages instead of putting them into the oven.)

Calories: 370 Sugar: 1 g Fat: 21 g Carbohydrates: 3 g Fiber: 1 g Protein: 40 g

FOR AIP: ensure your bacon is compliant and omit egg

Garlic Roasted Shrimp with Zucchini Pasta

Serves: 4

Prep Time: 10 mins || Cook Time: 10 min

Cooking Type: Baking

Course: Main dish

This easy shrimp with zucchini pasta recipe is a great weeknight dinner — you can have it on the table in 20 minutes.

Ingredients

- 8 ounces peeled and deveined shrimp thawed if frozen
- 4 tablespoons olive oil
- 2 cloves garlic minced
- 1 lemon zested and juiced
- 1/4 teaspoon salt
- fresh ground pepper to taste
- 2 medium zucchini spiralized or sliced into thin strips for zucchini pasta

Instructions

1. Preheat oven to 400 degrees.
2. Add shrimp, olive oil, ghee, garlic, lemon zest, lemon juice, salt and pepper to the baking dish. Toss to coat shrimp.
3. Bake for 8-10 minutes, turning once. Cook until shrimp are pink and just cooked through, or until heated through if using pre-cooked shrimp.
4. Add the zucchini pasta, toss and serve.

Calories: 409kcal | Carbohydrates: 8g | Protein: 25g | Fat: 31g | Saturated Fat: 11g | Cholesterol: 324mg | Sodium: 1188mg | Potassium: 602mg | Fiber: 1g | Sugar: 5g | Vitamin A: 390IU | Vitamin C: 46.4mg | Calcium: 201mg | Iron: 3.1mg

Easy Paleo Broccoli Soup

Serves: 4

Prep Time: 5 mins || Cook Time: 10 min

Cooking Type: Baking

Course: Main dish

This quick recipe is deceptively simple, but it makes a rich creamy soup with a hint of garlic.

Ingredients

- 1 16-ounce bag plain frozen broccoli
- cloves garlic peeled
- cups chicken stock or vegetable stock
- 1 tablespoon ghee or olive oil
- sea salt to taste
- fresh ground pepper to taste
- organic extra virgin olive oil for garnish, optional

Instructions

1. Bring broccoli, garlic, and stock to a boil over medium-high heat. Cover, reduce heat and simmer 10 minutes.
2. Carefully transfer to Vitamix and puree until smooth (or puree with an immersion blender).
3. Add olive oil, season with salt and pepper, and blend to combine.

Calories: 99kcal | Carbohydrates: 6g | Protein: 4g | Fat: 5g | Saturated Fat: 2g | Cholesterol: 15mg | Sodium: 257mg | Potassium: 189mg | Sugar: 2g | Vitamin C: 1.1mg | Calcium: 8mg | Iron: 0.4mg

Easy Cauliflower Celeriac Soup with Bacon

Serves: 4

Prep Time: 5 mins || Cook Time: 20 min

Cooking Type: Simmering

Course: Main dish

A decadent creamy soup made with cauliflower and celery root.

Ingredients

- 1 16- ounce bag frozen cauliflower
- 1 cup peeled and chopped celeriac
- 2 cloves garlic peeled
- 3-1/2 cups chicken stock or vegetable stock
- 2 tablespoons olive oil
- fresh ground pepper to taste
- sea salt to taste
- 4 slices cooked and crumbled bacon
- fresh chives for garnish

Instructions

1. Bring cauliflower, celeriac, garlic and chicken stock to a boil over medium-high heat. Cover, reduce heat and simmer until vegetables are tender, 15-20 minutes.
2. Carefully transfer to Vitamix and puree until smooth.
3. Add olive oil, salt & pepper and blend to combine.
4. Top with bacon and chives.

Calories: 238kcal | Carbohydrates: 13g | Protein: 8g | Fat: 17g | Saturated Fat: 7g | Cholesterol: 36mg | Sodium: 349mg | Potassium: 615mg | Fiber: 3g | Sugar: 4g | Vitamin C: 61.6mg | Calcium: 49mg | Iron: 1.1mg

Sheet Pan Chicken Fajitas

Prep Time: 10 Mins // Cook Time: 25 Mins

Yield: 4

Recipe Type: Main dish

An easy, Whole30 compliant, one pan meal the whole family will enjoy!

Ingredients

- 3 tbsp avocado oil
- 1 red bell pepper
- 1 orange (or yellow) bell pepper
- 1 green bell pepper
- 1 medium onion
- 1-1.5 lbs chicken breasts
- 1.5 tsp cumin
- 2 tsp chili powder
- 1 tsp garlic powder
- 1 tsp paprika
- 1/2 tsp oregano
- 1 tsp sea salt
- 1/2 tsp black pepper
- 1/2 tsp red pepper flakes

Instructions

1. Preheat your oven to 400 degrees. Slice the peppers, onion, and chicken into thin strips (about 1/4-1/2 inch wide). Make sure the chicken pieces are of even thickness to prevent uneven cooking.
2. Put these pieces into a large bowl and add the avocado oil and spices. Mix together and spread out evenly on a parchment lined rimmed baking sheet.
3. Bake for 25-30 mins until cooked through and beginning to brown. Serve in tortillas, on top of a salad, or in a rice bowl with your favorite toppings. Enjoy!

One Pan Taco Skillet dinner

Prep Time: 5 mins || Cook Time: 20 mins

Yield: 3-4 servings

This one-pan taco skillet dinner is so easy to make for a weeknight meal! It's packed with veggies, healthy fats and protein, and amazing flavor.

Ingredients

- 1 lb ground beef
- 1 onion, diced
- 2 cup cauliflower rice (pre-riced or using a food processor)
- 1 cup zucchini, diced
- 1 cup kale, thinly sliced
- 1 tsp sea salt
- 2 tsp oregano
- 2 tsp garlic powder
- 1/4 tsp turmeric
- Juice of one lime

Toppings:

- Dairy-free sour cream
- 2 tbsp green onion, chopped
- 2 tbsp cilantro, chopped
- 1 avocado, diced
- 1/4 cup black olives, sliced
- 1 lime, quartered

Instructions

1. Using a large skillet, brown the ground beef over medium heat. Set aside and reserve the fat in the pan.
2. Saute the onion in skillet for 4-5 minutes or until translucent.
3. Add in the cauliflower rice and zucchini and saute until the cauliflower rice is lightly browned and the zucchini is softened.
4. Stir in the greens and the seasonings and saute until the greens are wilted.
5. Add the beef back in and cook for 2-3 minutes to combine the flavors.
6. Remove the heat and add the toppings. Season further to taste and serve!

One Pot lasagna Skillet

Prep Time: 5 || Cook Time: 20

Yield: 4 servings

This one pot lasagna features everything you love about lasagna without the grains or dairy! It's the perfect one pot meal for a busy weeknight that the whole family will love.

Ingredients

- 2 large zucchinis
- 1 lb ground beef
- 1 tsp salt, divided
- 2 tbsp avocado oil
- 1 white onion, diced
- 3 cloves garlic, minced
- 1 cup mushrooms, chopped
- 1 tbsp fresh basil, chopped
- 1 tbsp fresh parsley, chopped (plus extra for garnish if desired)
- 2 tsp dried oregano
- 1 cup spinach

Instructions

1. Chop the ends off of the zucchinis, and use a mandolin slicer or a peeler to slice the zucchinis into long, thin strips. Pat them down with paper towels to remove excess water and set aside.
2. Use a large, deep skillet to brown the ground beef. Season with 1/2 tsp sea salt, and set aside and drain excess fat when cooked.
3. Add the oil to the pan and heat. Cook the onions and garlic in the same pan on medium heat until the onions are translucent. Add in the mushrooms, zucchini slices and saute for 4-5 minutes or until soft.
4. Add back in the ground beef, as well as the marinara sauce, and the remainder of the seasonings. Cook for a few minutes to combine the flavors, and stir in the spinach at the very end. Stir until the spinach has wilted.
5. Top with extra seasoning to taste, and serve!

Chicken and Shrimp Stir Fry

Prep Time 5 minutes||**Cook Time** 20 minutes

Servings: 6 people

Calories 322kcal

There's always time to whip up a quick stir fry! Here's a recipe with chicken, shrimp, and broccoli that's AIP paleo, keto, and low carb friendly.

Ingredients

1. 2 tablespoons lard or coconut oil
2. 1 small onion sliced thin
3. 4 cloves garlic minced
4. 3 tablespoons ginger minced

5. 1 pound broccoli cut into florets
6. 1 pound chicken skinned, boned, and cubed
7. 1/4 cup coconut aminos
8. 10 drops liquid stevia
9. 1 pound shrimp fresh or frozen, peeled with tails
10. 1/4 teaspoon sea salt

Instructions

1. In a large skillet or wok, melt the lard (or coconut oil) over medium-high. Add onions and cook until translucent. Stir in the garlic and ginger and stir fry until fragrant.
2. Dump in the broccoli and stir fry for about 10 minutes.
3. Add the coconut aminos and stevia. Then, stir in the chicken, shrimp, and salt. Cook until shrimp is heated throughout (or turns pink if using uncooked). Serve hot over cauliflower rice.

Amount Per Serving (0.17 recipe)

Calories 322 Calories from Fat 153

Fat 17g26%, Saturated Fat 4g25%, Cholesterol 247mg82%, Sodium 989mg43%, Potassium 481mg14%, Carbohydrates 9g3%, Fiber 2g8%, Sugar 1g1%, Protein 31g62%, Vitamin A 575IU12%, Vitamin C 73.4mg89%, Calcium 160mg16%, Iron 2.9mg16%

Mongolian Beef

Prep Time: 5 mins || Cook Time: 15 minutes

Servings: 4 servings

Calories: 318kcal

This easy Keto and Whole30 Mongolian Beef is so much healthier and tastier than takeout and it only takes 20 minutes to make

Ingredients

- 1 lb flank steak sliced against the grain into thin, bite-sized pieces
- 1/2 tsp sea salt
- 2 tsp tapioca starch
- 1/4 cup avocado oil
- 4 garlic cloves minced
- 1 inch fresh ginger grated
- 1/3 cup coconut aminos
- 1/4 cup water
- 1 tsp fish sauce
- 1 bunch green onions cut into 2-inch pieces

Instructions

1. Season the beef with salt, then toss together.
2. Sprinkle with tapioca starch then toss until evenly covered.
3. Heat avocado oil in a skillet over medium high heat.
4. Working in batches, drop the beef in the oil a few at a time so the pieces aren't touching each other. Fry until dark and crispy, about 1 1/2 minutes on each side.
5. Remove from the skillet and set aside. Drain the oil from the skillet but leave about 1 tablespoon.
6. Add garlic, ginger, if using, into the same skillet.
7. Sauté until fragrant, about 1 minute.
8. Add coconut aminos, water, and fish sauce, and stir to combine.
9. Add the fried beef, and let it simmer for 3 minutes until the sauce is thickened.
10. Stir in green onions and simmer for 2 more minutes.
11. Remove from heat and stir in sesame oil.
12. Sprinkle with sesame seeds before serving with cauliflower rice.

Calories 318 Calories from Fat 180, Total Fat 20g 31%, Saturated Fat 4g 20%, Cholesterol 68mg 23%, Sodium 927mg 39%, Potassium 415mg 12%, Total Carbohydrates 6g 2%, Protein 24g 48%, Vitamin A 2.7%, Vitamin C 2.5%, Calcium 3.4%, Iron 10.5%

Basil Chicken Saute Recipe

Prep Time: 10 minutes || Cook Time: 15 minutes

Yield: 2 servings

Ingredients

- 1 chicken breast (0.5 lb or 225 g), minced or chopped very small
- 2 cloves of garlic, minced or finely diced
- 1 cup (1 large bunch) basil leaves, finely chopped
- 2 Tablespoons (30 ml) water
- 1 Tablespoon (15 ml) gluten-free tamari sauce (use coconut aminos for AIP)
- 1 Tablespoon (15 ml) avocado oil or coconut oil to cook in
- Salt to taste

Instructions

1. Add 1 Tablespoon of avocado or coconut oil into a large saucepan and add in the minced garlic. When the garlic has started to yellow, add in the optional diced chili.
2. Then add in the minced chicken.
3. Add in the water and cook until the chicken is cooked.
4. Add to the saucepan the tamari sauce and salt to taste.
5. Lastly, add in the basil leaves and mix it in. Serve with some Cauliflower White "Rice" for a delicious Asian dish that's Paleo, Keto, and AIP.

All nutritional data are estimated and based on per serving amounts.

Serving Size: 1 Large Plate Sugar: 1 g Fat: 10 g Carbohydrates: 3 g Fiber: 1 g Protein: 30 g

Creamy Pulled Pork Soup

Prep Time: 15 minutes || Cook Time: 30 minutes

Yield: 2 servings

Ingredients

- 2 tsp (10 ml) coconut or avocado oil
- 1 medium onion
- 8 cloves garlic
- 1 1/2 lbs (680 g) cauliflower
- 1 tsp (5 g) fine sea salt
- 7 cups (1680 ml) chicken or pork broth
- 2 tsp (2 g) dried oregano
- 2 1/2 cups (300 g) pulled pork

Instructions

SOFTEN:

1. Heat a saucepan or dutch oven over low-medium heat. Dice the onion, then smash and peel the whole garlic cloves.
2. Add the oil, diced onion and smashed garlic to the pan, stirring through the oil to coat.
3. Allow the onion and garlic to soften, stirring occasionally to avoid any burning or coloring. Meanwhile, chop the cauliflower into evenly sized florets and add to the pan along with the salt and broth.

4. Increase the heat to medium-high and bring the broth to a simmer. Cook until the cauliflower is fork tender, about 20 minutes.

BLEND:

1. Remove the pan from the heat (turn off the burner) and carefully transfer it to a trivet and use an immersion blender to blend everything together until you have a smooth, creamy soup base.
2. Add the oregano leaves and return the pan to the heat.

SIMMER:

1. Turn the heat to medium and bring the soup back up to a simmer. If the soup is thicker than you prefer, add a little extra broth until the soup is the texture that you like.
2. Add the pulled pork and cook until the pork is hot all the way through before serving.

Crispy Ginger Lime Chicken Wings

Prep Time: 15 mins || Cook Time: 70

Yield: 30

Crispy Baked Wings, Tangy Sticky Sauce!

Ingredients

- 15 pastured chicken wings (cut into 30 pieces)
- ½ tablespoon baking powder **(see AIP recipe in post)**
- 1 tablespoon fine salt
- 1 tablespoon granulated garlic
- 2 tablespoons avocado oil

FOR THE SAUCE

- 2 tablespoons avocado oil
- 3 tablespoons coconut aminos
- 2 tablespoons apple cider vinegar
- ¼ cup bone broth
- ¼ cup juice from the orange
- zest of orange
- zest of 2 limes
- 6 cloves garlic, zested
- 1 inch nub of ginger, zested
- 1 tablespoon nutritional yeast
- 1 teaspoon turmeric
- 1 teaspoon dried dill weed
- ½ teaspoon garlic powder
- ½ teaspoon ginger powder

Instructions

1. Pre-heat oven to 250F. Place a rack over a sheet pan and lightly oil it. Pat your chicken dry.
2. Cut your wings per the instructions above at both joints. Store the tips for later use like broth.
3. Put all of the drumettes and wingettes in a large bowl and toss with salt, garlic and baking powder. Drizzle in the oil and toss again.
4. Line all of the chicken pieces up on the rack, you might have to crowd them a little, but make sure none of the pieces are actually touching.
5. Bake at 250F for 35 minutes. Then crank the oven up to 425F degrees. Bake for another 45-50 minutes until crispy, golden and delicious.
6. While the wings bake, heat a small sauce pot over medium heat. Once it is hot add in the avocado oil, coconut aminos and apple cider vinegar.
7. Bring it to a simmer while you measure out the rest of the seasoning and zest the fruit.

8. Add the orange juice and broth to the mix and bring it to a simmer again until the liquid is reduced by half and lightly coats a spoon.
9. Mix in the zest, yeast and seasonings. Stir until the sauce is like a thick, kind of chunky glaze. Remove from the heat. Go relax, you have some idle time.
10. When the wings are done remove them from the oven and toss in a large bowl with the sauce! Serve hot and enjoy.

Recipe Notes:

Baking Powder, not baking soda, you will need baking powder, but do not let this deter you from this recipe. I learned early on in my AIP days to make my own baking powder and it's a no-brainer.

To create Baking Powder

- Mix EQUAL PARTS: baking soda, cream of tartar and arrowroot starch.
- The best way to do this is to sift them all together. I usually mix up about ½ cup of each and store for all my paleo, AIP and other baking needs.
- This baking powder works GREAT and it's totally allergen friendly!

Serving Size: 5, Calories: 450g, Fat: 38g, Carbohydrates: 5g, Fiber: 1g, Protein: 42g

White Chicken AIP Chili

Prep Time: 5 minutes || Cook Time: 25 minutes

Total Time: 30 minutes

Servings: 4 servings

Calories: 526kcal

This hearty and comforting White Chicken AIP Chili comes together in 30 minutes, and it's perfect for a delicious weeknight meal!

Ingredients

- 1 onion
- 2 celery stalks
- 4 garlic cloves
- 1 tbsp coconut oil
- 1.5 lbs boneless chicken thighs or breasts
- 1 tsp dried oregano
- 1 tsp onion powder
- 1 tsp garlic powder
- 1 tsp salt
- 4 cups bone broth
- 2 limes
- 1 14-oz can of full-fat coconut milk

Optional: cilantro, green onion, plantain chips, avocado for garnish

Instructions

1. Dice onion, chop celery, and mince garlic cloves.
2. Heat coconut oil over medium-high heat. Add onion, celery, and garlic and cook stirring for 5 minutes.
3. Push the veggies to the side then add the chicken.
4. Season with dried oregano, onion powder, garlic powder, and salt.
5. Cook for 5 minutes, until chicken is browned on all sides.
6. Add the bone broth to the pot and squeeze in juice from limes, and bring to boil.
7. Lower heat to medium-low, and simmer for 10 minutes.
8. Remove chicken and transfer to a bowl, then use 2 forks to shred it completely.
9. Add the chicken back to soup, then add coconut milk.
10. Increase heat to medium-high, then boil for 10 minutes until the soup is slightly reduced and thickened.
11. Garnish as desired.

Calories 526 Calories from Fat 306, Total Fat 34g 52%, Saturated Fat 25g 125%, Cholesterol 161mg 54%, Sodium 856mg 36%, Potassium 825mg 24%, Total Carbohydrates 14g 5%, Dietary Fiber 4g 16%,

Sugars 5g, Protein 44g 88%, Vitamin A 2.9%, Vitamin C 19.5%, Calcium 6.6%, Iron 18.8%

Crispy Bratwurst with Glazed Brussel Sprouts

Prep Time: 3 minutes || Cook Time: 12 minutes

Yield: 5

Serving Size: 1/5 Recipe

Fast and easy healthy recipe! The perfect whole foods keto meal, made in 15 minutes!

Ingredients

- 1/4 cup coconut oil, for frying
- 5 fully cooked, pork bratwurst
- 1 pound brussel sprouts
- 1 large sweet onion
- 3 tablespoons avocado oil
- 1/2 teaspoon fine salt
- 1/2 teaspoon garlic powder
- 3 tablespoons coconut aminos
- 1 tablespoon vinegar
- 1 teaspoon fish sauce
- 2 tablespoons pastured gelatin

Instructions

1. Heat two large skillets over medium heat.
2. While they come to temperature slice your bratwurst into thin slices, small dice the onion and shred the brussel sprouts (if not using pre-shredded).
3. Add coconut oil to one skillet and the avocado oil to another. Let the coconut oil heat for another minute or so. In the meantime, add the diced onion to the avocado oil skillet and saute for 2 minutes then add in the brussel sprouts.
4. Add the bratwurst to the coconut oil and fry, stirring occasionally for 8-10 minutes. Simultaneously saute the onion and brussel sprouts until they are browned and tender. Mix in the salt and garlic powder to the brussel sprouts.
5. In the small bowl combine the coconut aminos, vinegar and fish sauce, then add 2 tablespoons of gelatin on top and let it bloom. (Blooming gelatin: let it rest until the liquid has become a solid gel mass).
6. Lower the heat on the brussel sprouts and mix in the gelled sauce mass to the veggie mix. It will melt and create a thick glaze sauce. Remove from heat.
7. Turn off the heat on the bratwurst skillet. Use a slotted spoon to remove the crispy bratwurst from the coconut oil. Serve together right away. Great with some mustard on top!

Recipe Notes:

- To make this dish AIP: use AIP compliant bratwurst
- To make this dish Whole30: use Whole30 compliant bratwurst
- Time Saving Tip: Buy a bag of shredded brussel sprouts instead of slicing them yourself!

Calories: 522, Fat: 46g, Carbohydrates: 16g, Fiber: 3g, Protein: 15g

Healthy Chicken Finger Recipe

Prep Time: 15 mins || Cook Time: 25 mins

Course: Main Course

Servings: 4 Servings

Calories: 345 kcal

I created this gluten free and paleo chicken finger recipe so I could continue enjoying a healthier version of one of my favourite foods, and make something familiar for my family too. Plus, this recipe is AIP compliant, Whole30, keto, and kid-friendly to boot!

Ingredients

- ½ cup coconut flour
- 2 teaspoons poultry seasoning (for AIP sub for compliant spices like sage, thyme, salt and marjoram)
- ½ teaspoon sea salt
- 1 lb boneless skinless pastured chicken breasts
- ¼ cup avocado oil or melted ghee
- Coconut or avocado oil in a spray bottle (for misting)

Instructions

1. Preheat oven to 400F.
2. In a shallow bowl or on a plate, combine the coconut flour, poultry seasoning, and sea salt.
3. Slice the chicken breast into strips, and coat generously with avocado oil.
4. Dip the oil-coated chicken strips into the coconut flour mixture to coat.
5. Place the finished strips onto a baking sheet one-at-a-time. When all the strips are coated, mist them with a thin coating of oil (this step makes them even crispier).
6. Bake for 12 minutes, flip them over and mist with oil, before returning to the oven for another 12 minutes.
7. Enjoy with your favourite dip like organic ketchup or homemade paleo mayo!

Calories 345 Calories from Fat 198, Fat 22g34%, Saturated Fat 7g44%, Cholesterol 72mg24%, Sodium 454mg20%, Potassium 419mg12%, Carbohydrates 9g3%, Fiber 5g21%, Sugar 1g1%. Protein 26g52%, Vitamin A 60IU1%, Vitamin C 1.3mg2%, Calcium 16mg2%, Iron 1.2mg7%

Pressure Cooker Garlic "Butter" Chicken Recipe

Prep Time: 5 minutes || **Cook Time:** 40 minutes

Yield: 4 servings

Ingredients

- 4 chicken breasts, whole or chopped
- ¼ cup Coconut oil
- 1 teaspoon salt (add more to taste)
- 10 cloves garlic, peeled and diced

Instructions

1. Add the chicken breasts to the pressure cooker pot.
2. Add the oil, salt, and diced garlic to the pressure cooker pot.
3. Set pressure cooker on high pressure for 35 minutes. Follow your pressure cooker's instructions for releasing the pressure.
4. Shred the chicken breast in the pot.

Net Carbs: 3 g

Calories: 404 Sugar: 0 g Fat: 21 g Carbohydrates: 3 g Fiber: 0 g Protein: 47 g

keto lemon Blueberry Chicken salad

Prep Time: 10 minutes || Cook Time: 10 minutes

Yield: 1 serving

Category: Dinner

Ingredients

- 10 blueberries or other berries
- 1/4 medium onion, sliced
- Large bag of salad leaves (approx. 125 g)
- 2 Tablespoons (30 ml) olive oil
- 2 teaspoons (10 ml) fresh lemon juice
- 1 large chicken breast (1/2 lb), diced
- 2 Tablespoons (30 ml) coconut oil to cook in

Instructions

1. Sauté the diced chicken breast in 2 tablespoons of coconut oil. Add salt to taste.
2. Toss the cooked chicken with the blueberries, onion slices, salad leaves, olive oil, and lemon juice.

Serving Size: 1 large bowl Calories: 490 Sugar: 1 g Fat: 42 g Carbohydrates: 5 g Fiber: 3 g Protein: 27 g Net Carbs: 2 g

Aip Italian Burgers Recipe

Prep Time: 5 minutes || Cook Time: 10 minutes

Yield: 2 servings

Category: Lunch, Dinner

Grass-fed beef burgers are not only AIP, Paleo, and Keto, but they're also just really tasty and easy to make.

So, whip these up no matter what diet you're on. You can also switch out the seasonings or add in some vegetables to change the flavors.

Ingredients

- 1 lb of grass-fed ground beef (450 g)
- 2 Tablespoons of Italian seasoning (6 g)
- 2 Tablespoons of garlic powder (20 g)
- 1 Tablespoon of onion powder (7 g)

Instructions

1. Mix all the ingredients together well and form burger patties from the mixture.
2. Grill or pan-fry in coconut oil until done to your liking.

Calories: 640 Sugar: 3 g Fat: 48 g Carbohydrates: 9 g Fiber: 1 g Protein: 39 g

Sheet Pan Taco Bowls

Prep Time: 10 mins || Cook Time: 35 mins

Ingredients

FOR THE SHEET PAN

- 3 tablespoons avocado oil, divided
- 2 cups cauliflower rice, frozen
- 1 pound boneless skinless chicken thighs
- ½ red onion, sliced
- 1 bunch radishes, quartered
- 2 teaspoons pink Himalayan salt
- 1 teaspoon ground ginger
- 1 teaspoon dried parsley
- 1 teaspoon ground turmeric

FOR THE SAUCE

- 1 bunch cilantro, stems trimmed
- juice of 2 lemons
- 1 tablespoon apple cider or coconut vinegar
- 2 tablespoons coconut manna or coconut butter
- ½ teaspoon fine Himalayan salt
- 1 tablespoon nutritional yeast
- 1 tablespoon coconut aminos
- ½ cup avocado oil

TO SERVE

- 1 heart of romaine, shredded
- 1 ripe avocado, sliced

Instructions

1. Pre-heat the oven to 400F.
2. Drizzle one tablespoon of avocado oil all over a sheet pan.
3. One on side spread out 2 cups of frozen cauliflower rice.
4. Next to it, line up the chicken thighs so they are lying flat, snug but not overlapping.
5. In the space that is left arrange the red onion and radishes. Sprinkle the salt over everything, getting about 1 teaspoon on the chicken thighs.
6. Next add the remaining seasoning only to the chicken.
7. Then drizzle the rest of the oil all over the chicken and rice.
8. Put the sheet pan in the oven and roast for 30 minutes. Then broil for 5 minutes.
9. In the meantime, prepare the rest of the bowls. Shred the lettuce, slice the avocado and make the sauce.

10. Combine the cilantro, nutritional yeast, lemon juice, coconut manna, salt and coconut aminos in the blender, and blend on low until almost smooth. Then slowly drizzle in the avocado oil until the sauce is fluid. Remove from the blender and store in the fridge until ready to serve!
11. To assemble your bowls make a bed of romaine in two bowls. Then spoon the rice on one side, the radishes and onions on another. Find a spot for your avocado. Slice 2 chicken thighs per bowl. Then drizzle sauce over everything.
12. There will be extra sauce. Store it in the fridge and use as salad dressing!

Roasted "Loaded" Cauliflower

Prep Time: 35 mins || **Total Time:** 35 mins

Servings: 5 servings

Ingredients

- 2 heads cauliflower chopped small
- 10-12 ounces bacon
- 1 bunch green onions chopped, whites and greens separated into two piles
- 1 cup melting cheese (optional), grated leave out for AIP or if you can't have dairy; best options include fontina, Port Salut and jack
- 1 teaspoon sea salt
- several sprigs fresh thyme

Instructions

1. Preheat oven to 400 degrees Fahrenheit.
2. Spread bacon out on a large baking sheet (preferably a half sheet) Bake until done, about 15-20 minutes.
3. Remove bacon to plate, and set aside. Keep pan with fat.
4. Spread out cauliflower on pan with bacon fat. Sprinkle with sea salt. Toss well with two spoons, so cauliflower is well-coated with fat. (*At this point, if you wish to make a one-pan dinner with roasted chicken, see instructions below in Recipe notes.)

5. Roast cauliflower about 22 minutes, or until tinged with brown on its edges.
6. Remove pan from oven. Add green onions' whites and optional cheese. Reduce oven temp to 200 degrees.
7. Put back in oven for 5 minutes.
8. Remove from oven. Transfer to serving dish with any pan juices. Top with green onions' greens and fresh thyme. Serve.
9. For individual servings, plate individual portions, top with green onions and thyme, and top with optional fried eggs for main course dish. For egg-free and AIP option, top with simple roasted chicken and serve with side salad.

Recipe Notes

- If you wish to roast chicken to make a one-pan dinner, we'll use the same bacon pan after Step 4: so...toss cauli in bacon fat with sea salt as Step 4 directs. Then put this cauli aside in a large bowl.
- Spread chicken legs (bone in, skin on, about 1.5 lbs) out on baking sheet. Roll them over a bit in the fat. Sprinkle with sea sal. Reduce heat to 375, and bake 10 minutes.
- Remove pan; increase oven temp to 400. Spread cauli on baking sheet all around chicken pieces, using a spatula to scrape any extra fat from bowl onto chicken pieces, basting them.
- Resume recipe with Step 5, baking cauli for about 22 minutes...

Creamy Tarragon Chicken Salad

Prep Time: 30 mins ||

Serves: 2 Servings

Serving size: 1 serving

Ingredients

- 3 cups white chicken meat, chopped
- ¼ cup avocado oil
- 2 tbsp sherry vinegar
- 2 medium pears (1 1/2 cup total)
- ¼ cup red onion, 1/4th inch dice
- 2 tbsp fresh tarragon, minced
- 1 tsp sea salt

Instructions

1. Place chopped chicken in a large mixing bowl.
2. Mince the tarragon and add to the bowl, along with the pomegranate seeds if using.
3. Peel and chop the pears, placing 1/2 cup into the mixing bowl.
4. Blend remaining 1 cup of chopped pear, avocado oil, sherry vinegar, and sea salt until thick and smooth.
5. Pour the dressing over the chicken and toss around in the bowl until evenly coated then serve over a bed of leafy greens.

Chicken Casserole with Broccoli and Olives

Prep Time: 10 minutes || Cook Time: 75 minutes

Yield: 6 servings

Category: Dinner, Lunch

Ingredients

- 2 chicken breasts (400 g), diced
- 2 heads of broccoli (900 g), broken into small florets
- 1 medium onion (110 g), diced
- 20 white button mushrooms (200 g), diced
- 6 slices of bacon, diced and cooked (optional – make sure to get AIP compliant bacon)
- 20 olives, sliced
- 1–2 cups of coconut cream (240 ml), to cover the dish
- 3 Tablespoons of coconut oil (45 ml), to cook chicken in
- Salt, to taste

Instructions

1. Preheat oven to 350 F (175 C).
2. Cook the chicken breast in the coconut oil in a frying pan. Season with salt.
3. Add everything to a large baking pan and bake uncovered for 1 hour.

NOTES

All nutritional data are estimated and based on per serving amounts.

Calories: 472 Sugar: 5 g Fat: 35 g Carbohydrates: 15 g Fiber: 6 g Protein: 24 g

Easy Vegetable Beef Soup

Prep Time 10 minutes || Cook Time 8 hours

Servings 8 people

Calories 223kcal

Craving something hearty and warming? And doesn't take a lot of prep time?
Learn how to make this easy beef soup with vegetables, based on a Filipino
recipe.

Ingredients

- 2 pounds beef shank 4 slices, 1 inch thick per slice, bone in
- 400 grams red radish cut in half
- 600 grams napa cabbage (aka wombok) cut in half
- 300 grams eggplant sliced
- 6 cups beef broth
- 1 small onion chopped
- 3/4 teaspoon garlic powder
- 1/2 teaspoon Himalayan pink salt

Instructions

1. Wash beef in cold running water. Pat dry with paper towel.
2. Season beef with garlic, salt. Let it sit for 30 minutes, either at room
   temperature or in the fridge.

3. Place half of onions at the bottom of the slow cooker. Add 2 slices of beef, top with onions, add the remaining beef and onions. Pour beef broth.
4. Cook on high for 7 to 8 hours until beef is tender and falling off the bones.
5. Add radishes 30 minutes to one hour plus the eggplants and napa cabbage 15 to 30 minutes before turning off the slow cooker. Length of cooking the vegetables will depend on how soft you want them to be.
6. Enjoy this hearty soup with Eggplant Ensalata on the side and opt for some cauliflower rice.

Notes

- Look for beef shank with marbling bone marrow which adds flavor to the soup.
- Cut beef into bite sized pieces to cook faster.

Calories 223 Calories from Fat 45, Fat 5g8%, Saturated Fat 1g6%, Cholesterol 49mg16%, Sodium 1112mg48%, Potassium 984mg28%, Carbohydrates 11g4%, Fiber 3g13%, Sugar 6g7%, Protein 31g62%, Vitamin A 245IU5%, Vitamin C 34.2mg41%, Calcium 127mg13%, Iron 3.8mg21%

Caramelized Balsamic Leek Turkey Hearts

Prep Time: 30 mins || Cook Time: 5 mins.

Serves: 2 servings

Serving size: 1 serving

Ingredients

- 8 oz turkey hearts
- 1/4 cup olive oil
- 3/4 tsp sea salt
- 2 tbsp balsamic vinegar
- 3 cups leek greens – chopped
- Fresh basil for garnish.

Instructions

1. Prepare turkey hearts by cutting each heart into fourths.
2. Heat 2 tbsp olive oil in a large pan over medium heat, and once hot, add leeks and allow-ing them to cook until tender and fragrant.
3. Remove cooked leeks from the pan and set aside for later use, then add remaining 2tbsp olive oil to the pan, turning the heat to low.
4. Add prepared turkey hearts to the pan, sprinkle with remaining sea salt and cover, allow-ing them to cook for 2-3 minutes until no longer pink in the middle.

5. Add the cooked leeks back into the pan and deglaze the pan with the balsamic vinegar,quickly stirring to scrape up any crispy bits from the bottom of the pan, then take the pan off the heat and serve, topping with basil sprigs.

Recipe Notes

- The basil is optional, but highly recommended, as it adds an extra pop of flavor especially loved by the individuals I served this dish to
- If you don't have turkey hearts, chicken hearts work equally as great.

Chicken Casserole with Broccoli and Olives

Prep Time: 10 minutes ||Cook Time: 75 minutes

Yield: 6 servings

Ingredients

- 2 chicken breasts (400 g), diced
- 2 heads of broccoli (900 g), broken into small florets
- 1 medium onion (110 g), diced
- 20 white button mushrooms (200 g), diced
- 6 slices of bacon, diced and cooked (optional – make sure to get AIP compliant bacon)
- 20 olives, sliced
- 1–2 cups of coconut cream (240 ml), to cover the dish
- 3 Tablespoons of coconut oil (45 ml), to cook chicken in
- Salt, to taste

Instructions

1. Preheat oven to 350 F (175 C).
2. Cook the chicken breast in the coconut oil in a frying pan. Season with salt.
3. Add everything to a large baking pan and bake uncovered for 1 hour.

Calories: 472 Sugar: 5 g Fat: 35 g Carbohydrates: 15 g Fiber: 6 g Protein: 24 g

Asian Stuffed Mushrooms Recipe

Prep Time: 15 minutes ||**Cook Time:** 15 minutes

Yield: 4 servings

Ingredients

For the mushrooms and stuffing:

- 20 medium white button mushrooms, remove the stem
- 1/2 lb (225 g) ground chicken (or use 1 chicken breast food processed)
- 2 green onions, finely chopped
- 2 cloves of garlic, minced
- 1 Tablespoon ginger, minced
- 2 Tablespoons coconut aminos (30 ml)
- 1 teaspoon salt

For the dipping sauce:

- 4 cloves of garlic, minced
- 4 Tablespoons of coconut aminos (60 ml)
- 1/2 teaspoon (2.5 ml) apple cider vinegar

Instructions

1. In a mixing bowl, combine the ground chicken, green onions, ginger, garlic, coconut aminos, and salt. Mix well.
2. Clean the mushrooms (remove the stems carefully). Using your hands stuff the meat mixture into the mushrooms.
3. You can either bake or steam these. (I steamed them for 15-20 minutes until the meat is cooked).
4. To make the dipping sauce, mix together the garlic, coconut aminos, and vinegar in a small bowl.
5. Serve the steamed stuffed mushrooms with the dipping sauce.

Calories: 105 Sugar: 6 g Fat: 2 g Carbohydrates: 12 g Fiber: 4 g Protein: 13 g

keto Lemon Blueberry Chicken Salad

Prep Time: 10 minutes ||Cook Time: 10 minutes

Yield: 1 serving

Ingredients

- 10 blueberries or other berries
- 1/4 medium onion, sliced
- Large bag of salad leaves (approx. 125 g)
- 2 Tablespoons (30 ml) olive oil
- 2 teaspoons (10 ml) fresh lemon juice
- 1 large chicken breast (1/2 lb), diced
- 2 Tablespoons (30 ml) coconut oil to cook in
- Salt

Instructions

1. Sauté the diced chicken breast in 2 tablespoons of coconut oil. Add salt to taste.
2. Toss the cooked chicken with the blueberries, onion slices, salad leaves, olive oil, and lemon juice.

Net Carbs: 2 g

Serving Size: 1 large bowl Calories: 490 Sugar: 1 g Fat: 42 g Carbohydrates: 5 g Fiber: 3 g Protein: 27 g

Granola

Prep Time: 10 minutes ||Cook Time: 10 minutes

Yield: 4 serving

Ingredients

- 2 cups fancy grade coconut flakes
- 1 heaping Tablespoon coconut oil
- 1 heaping Tablespoon coconut manna
- zest of an orange
- 1/2 teaspoon cinnamon
- 1 pinch salt

Instructions

1. Heat coconut oil and coconut manna until pourable. Mix in cinnamon and remove from heat.
2. In a bowl, add coconut flakes and drizzle the coconut oil mixture over it. Toss lightly with a spoon.
3. Add pinch of salt and zest the orange over the mixture and gently stir again.
4. On a parchment lined half pan (cookie sheet), evenly distribute the coconut flake mixture.
5. Bake in 350-degree oven for about 12-15 minutes. Be sure to stir a few times as it will quickly brown and when you stir the coconut it will help to evenly brown the mixture.
6. Remove from oven and let cool.

3-Ingredient Crispy Keto Chicken Thighs Recipe

Prep Time: 5 minutes || **Cook Time:** 40 minutes

Yield: 4 servings

Ingredients

- 12 chicken thighs (with the skin on)
- 4 Tablespoons of olive oil (60 ml) or avocado oil
- 2 Tablespoons salt (30 g)

Instructions

1. Preheat oven to 450F (230C).
2. Rub salt on each chicken thigh in the mixture and place on a greased baking tray. Make sure the thighs are not touching each other on the tray. Drizzle the olive oil or avocado oil over the chicken thighs.
3. Bake for 40 minutes until the skin is crispy.

Net Carbs: 0 g

Turkey Sausage, kale & Pumpkin Soup

Yield: Serves 8

Ingredients

- 1 lb sweet italian turkey sausage
- 1/2 cup chopped onion
- 3 cups chopped pumpkin or butternut squash
- 4 cups chopped kale
- 4 cups chicken broth
- 4 cups water

Instructions

1. Cook sausage in a medium sized saucepan. Add onions and saute until translucent. Pour the broth and water into the saucepan and bring to a boil – reduce heat.
2. Add the kale and pumpkin and simmer until the pumpkin is soft, about 20 minutes.

Calories: 118, Fat: 6g, Carbohydrates: 5.5g net, Protein: 11g

Leek and Cauliflower Soup with Coconut Cream

Prep Time: 10 mins || Cook Time: 1 hour

Yield: 4

Ingredients

- 1 large leek (approx 10 oz)
- 1/2 cauliflower (approx 10 oz)
- 1/2 cup coconut cream, warmed + 2 additional Tablespoons (30 ml) for drizzling
- 3 cups chicken or bone broth
- Salt to taste

Instructions

1. Cut the cauliflower and leek into small pieces.
2. Place the cauliflower and leek into a large pot with the chicken or bone broth (or use a pressure cooker).
3. Cover the pot and simmer for 1 hour or until tender.
4. Use an immersion blender to puree the vegetables to create a smooth soup. (If you don't have an immersion blender, you can take the vegetables out, let cool briefly, puree in a normal blender, and then put back into the pot.)
5. Add in the coconut cream and salt to taste and mix well.

Easy Zucchini Beef Saute with Garlic and Cilantro

Prep Time: 5 minutes || Cook Time: 10 minutes

Yield: 2 servings

Ingredients

- 10 oz (300 g) beef, sliced into 1–2 inch strips (against the grain if you can)
- 1 zucchini (approx. 300 g), cut into 1–2 inch long thin strips
- 1/4 cup cilantro, chopped
- 3 cloves of garlic, diced or minced
- 2 Tablespoon coconut aminos
- Avocado oil to cook with (coconut oil or olive oil)

Instructions

1. Place 2 tablespoons of avocado oil into a frying pan on high heat.
2. Add the strips+ of beef into the frying pan and saute for a few minutes on high heat.
3. When the beef is browned, add in the zucchini strips and keep sauteing.
4. When the zucchini is soft, add in the tamari sauce, garlic, and cilantro.
5. Saute for a few minutes more and serve immediately.

Serving Size: approx 300g Calories: 500 Sugar: 2 g Fat: 40 g Carbohydrates: 5 g Fiber: 1 g Protein: 31 g

Bacon-Beef Liver Pâté with Rosemary and Thyme

Prep Time: 20 Mins || Cook Time: 20 Mins

Serves: 2 cups

Ingredients

- 6 pieces uncured bacon
- 1 small onion, minced
- 4 cloves garlic, minced
- 1 pound grass-fed beef liver
- 2 tablespoons fresh rosemary, minced
- 2 tablespoons fresh thyme, minced
- ½ cup coconut oil, melted
- ½ teaspoon sea salt
- Slices of fresh carrot or cucumber

Instructions

1. Cook the bacon slices in a cast-iron pot until crispy. Set aside to cool, reserving the grease in the pan to cook the liver.
2. Add the onion and cook for 2 minutes on medium-high. Add the garlic and cook for a minute. Add the liver, sprinkling with the herbs. Cook for 3-5 minutes per side, until no longer pink in the center.

3. Turn off heat, and place contents into a blender or food processor with the coconut oil and sea salt. Process until it forms a thick paste, adding more coconut oil if too thick.
4. Cut the cooled bacon strips into little bits and mix with the pâté in a small bowl. Garnish with some fresh herbs and serve on carrot or cucumber slices.

Caramelized Balsamic Leek Turkey Hearts

Prep Time: 20 Mins || Cook Time: 20 Mins

Serves: 2 serve

Ingredients

- 8 oz turkey hearts
- 1/4 cup olive oil
- 3/4 tsp sea salt
- 2 tbsp balsamic vinegar
- 3 cups leek greens – chopped
- Fresh basil for garnish.

Instructions

1. Prepare turkey hearts by cutting each heart into fourths.
2. Heat 2 tbsp olive oil in a large pan over medium heat, and once hot, add leeks and allow-ing them to cook until tender and fragrant.
3. Remove cooked leeks from the pan and set aside for later use, then add remaining 2tbsp olive oil to the pan, turning the heat to low.
4. Add prepared turkey hearts to the pan, sprinkle with remaining sea salt and cover, allow-ing them to cook for 2-3 minutes until no longer pink in the middle.
5. Add the cooked leeks back into the pan and deglaze the pan with the balsamic vinegar,quickly stirring to scrape up any crispy bits from the

bottom of the pan, then take the pan off the heat and serve, topping with basil sprigs.

Recipe Notes

Thai Coconut Curry Shrimp Bowls

Prep Time: 15 Mins // Cook Time: 15 Mins

Yield: 4

Recipe Type: Main dish

The ultimate gluten and dairy-free comfort dish!

Ingredients

- 1 16 oz package frozen shrimp (peeled and deveined) Thawed for 5-7 minutes under cold running water
- 1 package Stir Fry Veggie Mix from Trader Joes or use whatever veggies you have on hand.
- 2 tbsp avocado or sesame oil divided
- 2 minced garlic cloves
- 2 tbsp thai red curry paste
- 1 can full fat coconut milk
- 1/2 tsp red pepper flakes
- juice from 1/2 lime
- salt to taste
- 1 package frozen caulirice (or regular rice if preferred)

Instructions

1. Heat 1 tbsp oil over medium high heat. Add shrimp and cook for 2 mins each side until no longer pink. Remove from pan and set aside.
2. In the same pan, add remaining tbsp oil and veggies. Sauté until they begin to soften, about 5-7 minutes. Add in minced garlic, red pepper flakes, and thai red curry paste. Stir for 1-2 minutes until fragrant.
3. Add in coconut milk and stir. Bring to a boil, then reduce heat to low and let it simmer while you may your caulirice.
4. For the caulirice, I just sauté it with 1 tbsp oil for 5-7 minutes until softened and cooked through. Add lime juice to the curry and stir well.
5. Serve the curry overtop the rice/veggie noodles and enjoy!

Whole30 Taco Skillet

Prep Time: 1 Mins // **Cook Time:** 15 Mins

Yield: 4-6

Recipe Type: Main dish

A quick & clean weeknight meal that comes together in just 15 minutes!

Ingredients

- 1 lb grass fed ground beef
- 1 package frozen cauliflower rice (I prefer this over fresh- better consistency - doesn't get mushy!
- 1 14.5 oz can diced tomatoes with green chilis
- 1 tsp avocado or olive oil
- 1.5 tbsp chili powder
- 1 tbsp cumin
- 1 tsp paprika
- 1 tsp oregano
- 1/2 tsp sea salt
- 1/4 tsp cayenne pepper
- 1 tsp garlic powder
- 1 tsp onion powder

Instructions

1   Brown the beef in a large sauté pan. Drain, remove from the pan, and set
    aside. In the same pan, add the oil and heat over medium high heat.
2   Add the frozen cauliflower rice and cook for 4-5 mins until softened.
3   Add the beef back into the pan along with the tomatoes (with juices), and
    spices.
4   Stir to combine and cook for an additional 1-2 minutes until heated
    through. Serve with avocado, cilantro, and hot sauce. Enjoy!

Paleo Shrimp Fried Rice

A Whole30 & grain free version of your favorite Chinese takeout dish - gluten free, soy free, and MSG free!

Prep Time: 5 Mins // Cook Time: 15 Mins

Yield: 4-6

Recipe Type: Main dish

Ingredients

- 2 bags frozen cauliflower rice I like this better than fresh - it doesn't get as mushy!
- 1 bag frozen carrot/peas mix
- 1/2 onion diced
- 2 cloves garlic minced
- 1 egg
- 1 bag frozen (or fresh) shrimp I like the bag of raw/tail-on frozen shrimp from Trader Joe's
- 2 tbsp sesame oil
- 1 tsp rice vinegar
- 1 tsp ground ginger
- 1/2 tsp red pepper flakes
- 1/2 tsp fish sauce
- 1/4 cup coconut aminos
- chopped green onions for garnish

Instructions

1. Thaw and remove tails from shrimp. Heat a large skillet over medium high heat and add 1 tbsp sesame oil.
2. When hot, add shrimp and cook for ~ 2 mins each side with a bit of salt & pepper. Remove from the pan.
3. Add the remaining 1 tbsp sesame oil to the pan and add in the frozen cauliflower, carrots, peas, onion, and garlic. Sauté/cook until heated through, about 5-7 minutes.
4. Push the veggies to one side of the pan and use the other side to scramble your egg. Crack it and use a spatula to quickly scramble/cook the egg, then mix it all together.
5. Add the shrimp back into the pan along with the remaining ingredients. Stir and bring to a boil, and cook an additional 2-3 minutes or until any extra liquid cooks off. Serve and enjoy!

Instant Pot Keto Smothered Pork Chops

Serves: 4

Prep Time: 6 mins || Cook Time: 15 min

Cooking Type: Pressure Cooking

Serving size: One 5.2-ounce pork chop.

Course: Main dish

These tasty Instant Pot Keto Smothered Pork Chops are gluten-free, low carb, paleo, and have a whole30 (dairy free) option. Savory seared pork chops smothered in a creamy sauce with bacon, garlic, and mushrooms.

Ingredients

- 4 bone-in or boneless average cut pork loin chops (about 1.3 lbs)
- 2 slices uncooked bacon chopped
- 1 tsp dried thyme
- ½ tsp fine ground sea salt
- ¼ tsp ground black pepper
- 1½ tablespoon avocado oil or olive oil
- 2 cloves garlic minced
- ⅔ cup sliced white mushrooms
- 1 cup beef broth or bone broth
- ½ tsp onion powder
- ½ full-fat coconut milk
- ½ tsp garlic powder
- ½ tbsp teaspoon fresh thyme leaves or minced fresh parsley to garnish

Instructions

1   Sprinkle each side of pork chops with thyme, salt, and pepper. Press Sauté and add the avocado oil or olive oil to the inner pot. Heat until the pot shows "hot" on the screen.
2   Sear the pork chops on both sides for 2 to 3 minutes to just brown the sides in the inner pot. Remove the pork chops from the pot and set aside on a plate.
3   While still hot add the chopped bacon, minced garlic, and sliced mushrooms to the pot and sauté for about 3 to 4 minutes until the garlic has softened and bacon is browning.
4   Add the beef broth to the pot and scrape the bottom of the pot to deglaze. Stir in the onion powder and garlic powder. Press "Cancel" to turn off sauté mode.
5   Add pork chops back to the pot. Secure and lock the lid. Turn the pressure release handle to Sealing.

6   Select Pressure Cook on High Pressure (normal) and set the timer for 10 minutes for bone-in chops or 7 minutes for boneless chops by pressing the + or - buttons.

7   Once cooking time is done, let the pressure Naturally Release for 10 minutes (don't touch anything for 10 minutes), then Quick Release the remaining pressure (carefully while keeping face away from steam and hands in protective oven mitts, turn steam release handle to Venting).

8   Once all steam has released (the pin on the lid will drop and the lid will unlock), open the lid and remove only the pork chops, plate & cover to keep warm. Leave the mushrooms bacon and sauce in the pot and select Sauté and heat until bubbling.

9   Add the heavy cream or coconut milk to the sauce and stir. Continue to heat on sauté until bubbling. Press "Warm" on the pot. Plate pork chops and pour the mushroom bacon sauce over the chops garnish with fresh thyme leaves or fresh parsley.

Amounts per serving: Net Carbs per serving: 2g

Calories 452 Calories from Fat 306

Fat 34g52%, Saturated Fat 11g55%, Polyunsaturated Fat 1g, Monounsaturated Fat 8g, Sodium 422mg18%, Carbohydrates 2g1%, Sugar 1g1%, Protein 33g66%

Paleo Chicken Broccoli "Rice" Casserole

Serves: 6

Prep Time: 5 mins || Cook Time: 45min

Cooking Type: Baking

Course: Main dish

This creamy Paleo chicken, broccoli, and rice casserole is packed with flavor and filling in the best way! It's Whole30 compliant, keto, dairy free and perfect to make ahead of time for easy lunches and dinners.

Ingredients

sauce:

- 3 Tbsp ghee or rendered bacon fat **(Make sure it is AIP)**
- 1 med onion chopped
- 4 cloves garlic minced
- 2 Tbsp tapioca flour or arrowroot starch
- 1 3/4 cups chicken bone broth
- 1/2 cup coconut milk full fat
- 1 Tbsp spicy brown mustard
- 2 Tbsp nutritional yeast optional
- 1/4 sea salt or to taste
- 1/8 tsp black pepper or to taste
- 1 tsp fresh minced sage leaves
- 1 tbsp fresh minced rosemary

Remaining ingredients:

- oz cauliflower "rice" - I purchase this already prepped to save time
- 1 lb boneless skinless chicken breasts
- 1 lb broccoli florets
- 3 Tbsp avocado oil or olive oil, divided
- Sea salt and pepper
- 1/2 lb nitrate free bacon (sugar free)

Instructions

1. Preheat your oven to 425 degrees. Place chicken on a baking sheet and coat with 1 1/2 Tbsp olive oil and sprinkle with salt and pepper.
2. On a separate baking sheet lined with parchment paper, arrange broccoli and toss with 1 1/2 Tbsp avocado oil plus salt and pepper.
3. Roast chicken for 20-25 minutes or until cooked through. Midway through, flip the chicken and for even roasting. Roast broccoli for 15-20 mins or until fork tender, stirring midway through.
4. Once done, lower the oven temp to 400 degrees.

5   While chicken and broccoli roasts, cook bacon until crisp in a large skillet, drain, and make the sauce:
6   For the sauce, heat a medium saucepan over med heat and add the 3 Tbsp cooking fat. Add the onions, cook until translucent and fragrant, then add the garlic and continue to cook until soft, adjusting heat if necessary.
7   Whisk the tapioca flour into the broth and add it to the pan, then immediately add the coconut milk, mustard and nutritional yeast, (if using), while whisking. Raise the heat and bring to a boil, stirring.
8   Once boiling, lower to a simmer and continue to stir and cook for another minute, until nice and thick. Stir in salt and pepper to taste, add the fresh herbs. Stir in the cauliflower rice to soften, then remove from heat.
9   Cut the chicken into bite size pieces, or shred, and arrange in a casserole dish, then add the roasted broccoli and the sauce/rice mixture, stir to evenly coat.
10 Crumble the cooked bacon and sprinkle all over, then bake in the preheated oven for about 20 minutes, until heated through and cauli rice is soft. Serve hot and enjoy!

Calories: 479kcalFat: 36gSaturated fat: 14gCholesterol: 92mgSodium: 438mgPotassium: 889mgCarbohydrates: 12gFiber: 4gSugar: 3gProtein: 28gVitamin A: 510%Vitamin C: 97.8%Calcium: 65%Iron: 2.1%

Roasted Asparagus Avocado Soup

Serves: 4

Prep Time: 10 mins || Cook Time: 10 min

Cooking Type: Baking

Course: Main dish

Serving Size: 1/8th frittata

Avocado replaces the cream and makes the soup luxuriously silky.

Ingredients

- 12 ounces asparagus
- 1 tablespoon garlic infused olive oil
- 2 cups chicken stock or vegetable stock
- 1 avocado peeled and cubed
- 1/2 lemon juiced
- 1 tablespoon coconut oil
- sea salt to taste
- fresh ground pepper to taste

Instructions

1. Preheat oven to 425 degrees. Or preheat the air fryer to 390 degrees.
2. Toss asparagus with garlic infused olive oil, salt and pepper and roast for 10 minutes.
3. Carefully transfer asparagus to Vitamix or high-speed blender with remaining ingredients and puree until smooth. Add salt and pepper to taste.
4. Add water to thin to desired consistency, if needed, and warm gently over medium heat. Serve immediately.

Calories: 208kcal | Carbohydrates: 13g | Protein: 6g | Fat: 16g | Saturated Fat: 4g | Cholesterol: 13mg | Sodium: 177mg | Potassium: 560mg | Fiber: 5g | Sugar: 4g | Vitamin A: 715IU | Vitamin C: 17.2mg | Calcium: 34mg | Iron: 2.4mg

Easy Smoked Shrimp Recipe

This easy smoked shrimp recipe can be done in a smoker or with indirect heat on a grill.

Serves: 4

Prep Time: 5 mins || **Cook Time:** 20 mins

Cooking Type: Baking

Course: Main dish

Ingredients

- 1 pound shrimp deveined
- 1 tablespoon garlic infused olive oil
- sea salt to taste
- fresh ground pepper to taste
- 1/4 cup olive oil melted
- 1 clove garlic minced
- 1 tablespoon fresh basil and/or parsley minced

Instructions

1. Preheat smoker or grill and add wood chips according to manufacturer's instructions.
2. Toss shrimp with olive oil, salt and pepper.
3. Lay shrimp on smoker rack in a single layer and close the lid. Check shrimp after 10 minutes and keep a close eye on them. Smoke shrimp until just cooked through, about 15-20 minutes total.
4. While shrimp are smoking, combine butter, garlic, herbs and salt to taste. Drizzle over cooked shrimp and toss to coat. Serve remaining garlic herb butter as a dipping sauce.

Calories: 244kcal | Carbohydrates: 0g | Protein: 23g | Fat: 16g | Saturated Fat: 7g | Cholesterol: 314mg | Sodium: 881mg | Potassium: 90mg | Sugar: 0g | Vitamin A: 25IU | Vitamin C: 4.9mg | Calcium: 164mg | Iron: 2.4mg

Chili Lime Paleo Pork Ribs

Serves: 3

Prep Time: 5 mins || Cook Time: 3 hrs.

Cooking Type: Baking

Course: Main dish

Deliciously addicting Whole30 and paleo pork ribs, baked covered in chili lime dry rub. It's so tender and crispy, you won't be able to stop eating it!

Ingredients

- 2 lb pork spare ribs
- 1 tbsp avocado oil
- 1 tbsp chili powder
- 1 tsp paprika
- 1/2 tsp garlic powder
- 1/2 tsp sea salt
- 1/4 tsp ground black pepper **(Omit For AIP)**
- 1/4 tsp cayenne**(Omit For AIP)**
- Zest of 2 limes

Instructions

1. Preheat oven to 300 degrees F.
2. Rub avocado oil all over the spare ribs.
3. Mix the rest of the ingredients in a small bowl.
4. Sprinkle and press in the mixed rub all over the spare ribs so they are evenly coated.
5. Place a roasting rack over a baking pan.
6. Lay the spare ribs on the roasting rack and bake for 2.5-3 hours until they are juicy in the inside, and crispy on the outside.
7. Cut spare ribs into sections before serving.

Serving: 1serving | Calories: 639kcal | Carbohydrates: 2g | Protein: 33g | Fat: 54g | Saturated Fat: 16g | Cholesterol: 169mg | Sodium: 603mg | Potassium: 581mg | Fiber: 1g | Vitamin A: 24.6% | Calcium: 4.1% | Iron: 14.2%

Unstuffed Cabbage Roll Soup (Low Carb)

Gluten-Free, Dairy-Free

Prep Time 15 minutes // Cook Time 40 minutes

Servings: 8 servings

Calories 160 kcal

Simple comfort food: an easy recipe for unstuffed cabbage roll soup with beef, tomatoes, and other veggies.

Ingredients

- 28 ounce can diced tomatoes
- 1 pound 90% lean ground beef
- 1 pound chopped green cabbage (about 5 cups)
- 5 cups beef stock
- 1 cup rice cauliflower
- 1/2 cup diced onions
- 1/2 cup diced carrots
- 1 tablespoon olive oil
- 1 1/2 teaspoons salt
- 1 teaspoon dried oregano
- 1 teaspoon dried thyme
- 2 tablespoons fresh chopped parsley

Instructions

1. Heat a 6 quart pot or Dutch oven over medium to medium-high heat. Add olive oil and ground beef, cooking for a few minutes until browned, breaking it apart as it cooks.
2. Add onions and carrots. Cook for a few minutes to soften, stirring frequently.
3. Add tomatoes (including the liquid in the can), cabbage, beef stock, cauliflower, oregano, thyme, and salt. Stir everything together.
4. Increase heat to bring to a simmer. Cover with a lid and decrease heat to maintain a simmer. Simmer for about 30 minutes or until cabbage is tender.
5. Uncover and stir. Top with parsley and serve while hot.

This recipe yields 6 g net carbs per serving.

Calories 160, Total Fat 7g 11%, Saturated Fat 3g 14%, Trans Fat 0g. Cholesterol 38mg 13%, Sodium 1080mg 45%, Potassium 110mg 3%, Total Carb 8g 3%, Dietary Fiber 2g 7%, Sugars 5g. Protein 13g, Vitamin A 22% · Vitamin C 48% · Calcium 3% · Iron 12%

Paleo Beef with Broccoli

Paleo, Gluten-Free, Nut-Free, Dairy-Free

Prep Time: 15 Mins // Cook Time: 10 Mins

Servings: 4 People

Recipe Type: Main

Ingredients

- 1 lb. beef (sirloin, skirt steak, boneless short ribs...etc.)
- 1 to 2 heads broccoli, break into florets
- 2 cloves garlic, minced
- 2 pieces thin sliced ginger, finely chopped
- Ghee or cooking fat of your choice

Beef marinade:

- 2 tbsp. coconut aminos
- 1/2 tsp. coarse sea salt
- 1 tbsp. sesame oil
- 1/4 tsp. black pepper
- 1 tsp. arrowroot/sweet potato powder
- 1/4 tsp. baking soda

Sauce combo:

- 2 tbsp. coconut aminos
- 1 tbsp. red boat fish sauce
- 2 tsp. sesame oil
- 1/4 tsp. black pepper

Instructions

1. Slice beef into about ¼ inch thin. Marinate thin sliced beef with ingredients under "beef marinade". Mix well. Place broccoli florets in a microwave safe container. Add 1-2 tbsp. water. Loosely covered with a lid or wet paper towel and microwave for 2 mins. Cook until broccoli is tender but still crunchy. Set aside.
2. Heat a wok over medium heat w/ 1 ½ tbsp. ghee. When hot, lower the heat to medium, add garlic and ginger. Season w/ a small pinch of salt & stir-fry until fragrant (about 10 secs).
3. Turn up the heat to medium-high, add marinated beef. Spread beef evenly over the bottom of the sauté pan and cook until the edge of the beef is slightly darkened and crispy. Do the same thing for flip slide - about ¾ way cooked through with slightly charred and crispy surface.
4. Add "Sauce Combo". Stir-fry about 1 min. Add broccoli. Stir-fry another 30 secs. Toss everything to combine.

French Fries" Keto

Dairy-Free, Gluten-Free, Sugar-Free, Soy-Free, Nut-Free

Prep Time: 15 Mins // Cook Time: 35 Mins

Servings: 6

Recipe Type: Main

Ingredients:

- A bag of Parsley Root
- 1 1/2 Tsp. Pink Himalayan Salt
- 1 1/2 Tsp. Paprika
- 1 1/2 Tsp. Garlic Powder
- 1 Tsp. Onion Powder

Instructions:

1. Add cold water in a bowl and set aside.
2. Slice the Parsley Root as thin or thick as you like. (I like to slice mine pretty thin)
3. After you slice the parsley root, put in the bowl filled with water.
4. Leave it aside for an hour.
5. Strain and put on Parchment paper, add your seasoning, Drizzle with Avocado oil and Bake on 350F for about 30-40 minutes (Please check to see if done and crispy.
6. Please check every 10-15 minutes and turn fries so it can bake and crisp up throughout.
7. To Fry: make sure you fry the Parsley root till nice and golden in color with Avocado Oil, then add your seasoning.

You can also use these Root vegetables to make fries:

Please note: Oils that have high smoke points are suitable for cooking (Avocado Oil, Coconut Oil, Macadamia Oil, Lard etc. When looking for ingredients, try to get them in their more natural form (Organic, without any unnecessary additives).

London broil with Toasted Coconut Brussels

Dairy-Free, Gluten-Free, Sugar-Free, Soy-Free, Nut-Free

Prep Time: 10 Mins // Cook Time: 42 Mins

Yield: 4

Serving Size: 1/4 Recipe

Recipe Type: Main

An easy yet elegant meal the entire family will love. This sheet pan meal uses London broil for an affordable steak dinner!

Ingredients

For the Marinade:

- 1 teaspoon fine salt
- 1/2 teaspoon ground black pepper (omit for AIP)
- 2 cloves garlic, minced
- 4 sprigs fresh thyme
- 2 tablespoons avocado oil

Meat:

- 1– 1 1/5 pound London broil

Brussels sprouts:

- 1 pound Brussels sprouts, halved
- 2 tablespoons avocado oil
- 1/2 teaspoon fine salt
- 1 teaspoon onion powder
- 4 slices bacon, chopped (I also use Butcher Box Bacon)
- 2 tablespoons coconut butter (I use this one)

Instructions

1. In a casserole mix all of the marinade ingredients. Add the meat and flip it around in the marinade to get it all over. Cover and set in the fridge overnight, turning over once before cooking (the morning of).
2. When ready to cook, remove the meat from the fridge, let it rest at room temperature in its marinade for an hour.
3. In the meantime, preheat oven to 400F.
4. Add your Brussels sprouts to a sheet pan, toss with oil, salt, and onion powder.
5. Arrange bacon pieces all over it and then distribute the coconut butter in little clumps all over everything.

6. Roast on the middle rack for 30 minutes at 400.
7. Leaving the Brussels sprouts in the oven, set oven to broil at the 30-minute mark, making sure your second oven rack is right under the broiler.
8. Add your London broil (in the casserole dish where it marinated- or move it to a sheet pan) and place it under the broiler. Cook for 4-5 minutes. Then use tongs to flip it over and cook it other 4-5 minutes.
9. Remove everything from the oven. Move the meat over to a cutting board. Let it rest for 8-10 minutes before slicing against the grain.
10. Transfer the meat to the sheet pan with the Brussels sprouts and set that bad boy on the dinner table. Dinner is ready! Dig in.

Calories: 298, Fat: 25g, Carbohydrates: 9g, Fiber: 3g. Protein: 12g

Creamy Ham Soup

Prep Time: 10 Mins // Cook Time: 50 Mins

Yield: 6 servings

Serving Size: 1/6 Recipe

Recipe Type: Main dish

Ingredients

- 1 large head cauliflower (4 cups florets)
- 3 cups bone broth
- 1 smoked ham hock or shank, bone in (about 1-2lbs)
- 2 bay leaves
- ¼ tsp. nutmeg (optional)
- 1 teaspoon onion powder (optional)

Instructions

1. Cut the cauliflower into 4-5 pieces. Place them in your slow cooker or pressure cooker. Add in the ham hock, bay leaves, nutmeg and broth. If the ham and/or cauliflower are protruding a lot from the broth, add in water until they are just submerged.
2. For Pressure Cooker: Set to HIGH FOR 50 MINUTES.
3. For Slow Cooker: Set to HIGH FOR 4 HOURS.
4. When it is done, the cauliflower should be tender and mostly falling apart.
5. Use tongs and/or a slotted spoon to fish out the ham hock. It will be falling apart too. Set it in a small bowl and shred it. Remove the bone and any large pieces of fat.
6. Transfer most of the liquid along with most of the cauliflower, aim for the bigger pieces, to your blender. Add in a few pieces of ham. Blend until almost smooth. It should be a beige color, with pearl sized cauliflower pieces and specks of pink.
7. Pour this mix back in to the slow cooker or pressure cooker, add in the shredded ham. Mix well. It should be creamy with chunks of cauliflower about the size of beans (you see!) and pieces of ham.
8. If you want the soup thicker or thinner you can add more broth or water, alternatively you can reduce it (bring it to a simmer until desired consistency is achieved).
9. Serve and salt to taste. As I mentioned above, the ham is pretty salty, asis the seedy seasoning. Add your toppings and salt as needed when you serve the soup.
10. Store in an airtight container in the fridge for up to a week.

Per serving (for 6 servings) Calories 349, Fat 23 g, Carbohydrate 5 g, Fiber 2 g, Sugars 2 g, Protein 34 g

One-Skillet Spinach Artichoke Chicken

Serves: 6

Prep Time: 5 mins || Cook Time: 35 min

Cooking Type: Baking

Course: Main dish

This spinach artichoke chicken is crispy, creamy, and packed with flavor! It's Paleo, Whole30 compliant, dairy free, and made all in one skillet. Great served alone or over cauliflower rice!

Ingredients

- 6 chicken thighs bone-in, skin-on
- Sea salt and and pepper to season chicken
- 1 tsp lemon garlic seasoning or garlic powder
- 2 Tbsp Olive oil
- 8 oz fresh spinach roughly chopped
- 14 oz can artichoke hearts roughly chopped
- 1/2 med onion chopped (or 1 small)
- 4 cloves garlic minced
- 3/4 cup chicken bone broth
- 1 Tbsp fresh lemon juice
- pinch crushed red pepper optional
- Sea salt and pepper to season veggies
- 1/4 cup coconut milk full fat, blended prior to adding
- 2 tsp spicy brown mustard
- 2 tsp tapioca flour or arrowroot

Instructions

1. Preheat your oven to 400 degrees and make sure ingredients are prepped and ready to go
2. Heat a large cast iron skillet (or any oven proof skillet) over med-high heat. Season chicken with salt, pepper, and lemon-garlic seasoning, rubbing in to coat skin.
3. Add 2 Tbsp olive oil to skillet, then brown chicken on both sides - about 3-4 minutes per side.
4. Once browned, remove chicken from skillet to a plate and lower heat to medium. Add 1 more tbsp ghee to melt only if you need to.
5. Add onions and cook one minute until softened, then garlic and cook 30 seconds. Add spinach in batches to wilt, then artichoke hearts, stir and continue to cook 3 minutes over med heat until softened and heated through. Season with crushed red pepper, salt, and pepper to taste, stir in broth* and lemon juice. Remove from heat.

6   Return chicken back to skillet, place skillet in preheated oven and bake 25 minutes, until cooked through, return skillet to stovetop.

7   Remove just the chicken from skillet with tongs to make the sauce. Whisk tapioca and mustard into coconut milk, then add to skillet and whisk to combine. Bring to a boil and allow to boil 2-3 minutes until thickened, stirring. Return chicken to skillet and serve with spinach artichoke sauce. Enjoy!

Calories: 359kcalFat: 26gSaturated fat: 10gCholesterol: 123mgSodium: 182mgPotassium: 660mgCarbohydrates: 9gFiber: 3gProtein: 22gVitamin A: 3740%Vitamin C: 15.7%Calcium: 67%Iron:

Creamy Tuscan Chicken {Paleo, Whole30, Keto}

Serves: 6

Prep Time: 10 mins || Cook Time: 20 min

Cooking Type: Baking

Course: Main dish

This creamy paleo tuscan chicken is a super-tasty one-skillet meal that's perfect for weeknights and full of flavor! Boneless, skinless chicken thighs are seared and cooked with a creamy sauce packed with spinach and sun-dried tomatoes. Paleo, dairy-free, Whole30, and Keto friendly!

Ingredients

- 1.5 lbs chicken thighs boneless and skinless
- 1 Tbsp coconut oil plus additional if needed
- Sea salt and pepper
- 1/4 tsp garlic powder
- 1/4 tsp onion powder
- 1 small onion chopped
- 4 cloves garlic minced
- 1 Tbsp tapioca flour or arrowroot
- 1 cup chicken bone broth
- 1/2 cup coconut milk full fat, blended before adding if needed
- 1/2 Tbsp stone ground mustard
- 1 1/2 Tbsp nutritional yeast optional
- 1 tsp Italian seasoning blend
- 1/4 tsp sea salt or to taste
- 1/8 tsp black pepper or to taste
- 2/3 cup sun dried tomatoes roughly chopped
- 1 1/2 cups baby spinach roughly chopped

Instructions

1. Season the chicken with sea salt, pepper, garlic, and onion powder. In a large skillet add the coconut oil and cook the chicken thighs on medium-high heat for 5-7 minutes on each side or until browned and no longer pink in center.
2. Remove chicken and set aside on a plate.
3. Add additional oil if necessary and cook the onions over medium heat until soft, then stir in the garlic and cook another 45 seconds.
4. Whisk in the tapioca or arrowroot, the add the broth and coconut milk. Stir to combine, then stir in the mustard, yeast, Italian seasoning, sea salt and pepper. Cook and stir over medium-high heat until it starts to thicken.

5   Add the spinach and sun-dried tomatoes and allow mixture to simmer until spinach is wilted and tomatoes are softened. Add chicken back to the skillet and simmer another 2 minutes. Serve over cauli rice, zucchini noodles, or with roasted potatoes. Enjoy!

Calories: 368kcalFat: 25gSaturated fat: 10gCholesterol: 111mgSodium: 253mgPotassium: 806mgCarbohydrates: 12gFiber: 2gSugar: 5gProtein: 23gVitamin A: 900%Vitamin C: 9.1%Calcium: 46%Iron: 3%

Garlic Roasted Shrimp with Zucchini Pasta

Serves: 2

Prep Time: 10 mins || Cook Time: 10 mins

Cooking Type: Baking

Course: Main dish

This easy shrimp with zucchini pasta recipe is a great weeknight dinner — you can have it on the table in 20 minutes.

Ingredients

- 8 ounces peeled and deveined shrimp thawed if frozen
- 2 tablespoons olive oil
- 2 tablespoons additional olive oil
- 2 cloves garlic minced
- 1 lemon zested and juiced
- 1/4 teaspoon salt
- fresh ground pepper to taste
- 2 medium zucchini spiralized or sliced into thin strips for zucchini pasta

Instructions

1. Preheat oven to 400 degrees.
2. Add shrimp, olive oil, ghee, garlic, lemon zest, lemon juice, salt and pepper to the baking dish. Toss to coat shrimp.
3. Bake for 8-10 minutes, turning once. Cook until shrimp are pink and just cooked through, or until heated through if using pre-cooked shrimp.
4. Add the zucchini pasta, toss and serve.

Calories: 409kcal | Carbohydrates: 8g | Protein: 25g | Fat: 31g | Saturated Fat: 11g | Cholesterol: 324mg | Sodium: 1188mg | Potassium: 602mg | Fiber: 1g | Sugar: 5g | Vitamin A: 390IU | Vitamin C: 46.4mg | Calcium: 201mg | Iron: 3.1mg

Lemon Chicken Piccata

Serves: 6

Prep Time: 10 mins || Cook Time: 20 mins

Course: Main dish

This savory lemon chicken piccata is made all in one skillet and couldn't be easier! Perfect for weeknights and the leftovers save well for lunch the next day. It's gluten free, paleo, low carb and keto.

Ingredients

- 1.5 pounds boneless skinless chicken breasts pounded to 1/2" thickness (or purchased thin-sliced)
- Sea salt and black pepper to taste
- 3 Tbsp topica flour
- 2 Tbsp tapioca flour
- 3 Tbsp ghee divided
- 4 cloves garlic minced
- 1 small onion chopped (about 1/2 cup)
- 1 cup chicken bone broth
- Juice of 1 lemon about 2 Tbsp
- 1/2 cup coconut cream blended before using (the cream is the thick part of a chilled can of coconut milk. It can also be purchased separately
- 1 1/2 tsp stone ground mustard optional
- 1/4 cup capers drained
- Sea salt and black pepper to taste

Instructions

1. Pound your chicken breast to 1/2" thickness, if necessary, and cut into cutlets. Season with sea salt and pepper on both sides.
2. Heat a large skillet over medium/medium-high heat. In a shallow bowl, mix together the almond flour and tapioca* for dredging. Add 2 Tbsp of the ghee to the skillet.
3. Once the ghee is heated, lightly dredge the chicken, one cutlet at a time, in the flour mixture, shake off the excess, and place in the skillet. Cook about 4 minutes on each side to cook through. The outside should be golden brown - adjust the heat if you need to to avoid over-browning. Remove the chicken to a plate and set aside.
4. Lower the heat to medium low and add the remaining ghee. Add onions, cook for a minute until translucent, then add the garlic. Cook and stir another minute, until softened. Add the broth and lemon juice, then raise the heat to medium and bring to a boil, stirring occasionally.
5. Cook for 3 more minutes, then stir in the coconut cream and the mustard (if using). Cook and stir another minute, then stir in the capers. Add the chicken back to the skillet, lower the heat to a simmer and simmer

another minute. Serve over sautéed cauliflower rice or veggie noodles. Enjoy!

Calories: 308kcalFat: 19gSaturated fat: 12gCholesterol: 92mgSodium: 365mgPotassium: 519mgCarbohydrates: 7gFiber: 1gSugar: 1gProtein: 28gVitamin A: 44%Vitamin C: 4%Calcium: 26%Iron: 1%

Chicken Marsala with Bacon

Serves: 6

Prep Time: 10 mins || Cook Time: 25 mins

Cooking Type: Stove Top

Course: Main dish

This one-skillet paleo chicken marsala is loaded with flavor! Juicy chicken, a creamy mushroom sauce and crispy, savory bacon make this a recipe you'll want over and over! It's dairy-free, gluten-free, Paleo, and Whole30 compliant.

Ingredients

- 6 slices nitrate free bacon
- 3 Tbsp rendered bacon fat divided
- 1 1/2 lbs boneless skinless chicken breasts thin sliced
- Sea salt and black pepper
- 2 Tbsp tapioca flour or arrowroot starch, divided
- 1 medium onion diced
- 8 oz baby Bella mushrooms or preferred mushrooms, sliced
- 3-4 cloves garlic minced
- Pinch sea salt and black pepper
- 1 cup chicken bone broth
- 1 1/2 Tbsp balsamic vinegar or preferred vinegar
- 2/3 cup coconut milk full fat, blended
- 1 Tbsp nutritional yeast optional
- 2 tsp stone ground mustard optional
- Fresh herbs for garnish

Instructions

1. In a large deep skillet, cook bacon on med-high heat until crisp, then remove and drain on paper towels.
2. Reserve bacon fat in a container, then wipe the skillet of burnt bits.
3. Return skillet to medium-high heat and add 2 Tbsp bacon fat (or preferred cooking fat. Place 3 Tbsp tapioca on a plate or in a very shallow bowl. Sprinkle chicken with sea salt and pepper on both sides.
4. Coat chicken in the tapioca and shake off excess, then add to the hot skillet. Allow one side to turn golden brown (about 3-4 mins) then flip. Repeat with all chicken, working in batches if necessary. You might need to add more cooking fat if frying the chicken in batches.
5. Once chicken is done, set aside and lower the heat to medium. Add the remaining 1 Tbsp bacon fat, then add the onions and cook until translucent.
6. Add the mushrooms and garlic, another pinch of salt and pepper, and continue to cook another 3-5 minutes to soften. Mix the 1 tsp tapioca into

the broth, then add broth to the skillet, along with the vinegar, coconut milk, mustard, and nutritional yeast.

7   Stir and bring to a boil, then lower heat to a simmer and add the chicken back in, simmering for 3-4 minutes to thicken the sauce. For the last minute, crumble the cooked bacon into the skillet to heat through.

8   Serve over cauli rice, veggie noodles or with roasted potatoes. Enjoy!

Calories: 390kcalFat: 24gSaturated fat: 11gCholesterol: 93mgSodium: 319mgPotassium: 745mgCarbohydrates: 12gSugar: 2gProtein: 30gVitamin A: 35%Vitamin C: 3.5%Calcium: 24%Iron: 1.7%

Paleo Greek Meatballs with Tzatziki

Serves: 8

Prep Time: 20 mins || Cook Time: 15 min

Cooking Type: Baking

Course: Main dish

These easy greek meatballs are perfectly flavorful and delicious dipped in a dairy-free paleo Tzatziki sauce! Great as an appetizer or as part of a meal over a greek salad. Paleo, Whole30, and keto friendly.

Ingredients

tzatziki sauce:

- 1 can full fat coconut milk chilled until liquid and solid separates completely, at least 6 hours

- 3 cloves garlic
- 1 med cucumber peeled seeded, and grated
- tbsp fresh squeezed lemon juice *
- Zest of 1 lemon
- 3 tbsp dill fresh, chopped
- 3/4 tsp fine grain sea salt *
- Black pepper to taste
- 1/2 tsp cumin *

meatballs:

- 1 Tbsp olive oil
- 1 lb grass fed ground beef
- 1/2 lb ground lamb pork (or use all beef, if preferred)
- 2 Tbsp tapioca flour **
- 1 large egg **(Omit For AIP)**
- 1/4 cup red onion grated
- 2 cloves garlic minced
- Zest of 1 lemon grated
- Juice of 1 lemon about 2 Tbsp
- 2 Tbsp fresh parsley minced
- 2 Tbsp fresh mint minced
- 1 tsp coriander
- 1 tsp cumin
- 3/4 tsp dried oregano
- 3/4 tsp sea salt
- 1/4 tsp fresh ground pepper

Instructions

make the tzatziki first:

1. Squeeze excess liquid out of the grated cucumber and add to the bowl of a food processor.
2. Discard the liquid part of the coconut milk so you are left with the solid cream, and add that to the processor as well, along with the remaining ingredients.
3. Pulse/process until fully combined - it won't be completely smooth. Transfer to a bowl or container and refrigerate while you make the meatballs.

For the meatballs:

1. Preheat your oven to 450 degrees F and drizzle olive oil on a large baking sheet.
2. Combine all meatball ingredients (except olive oil) well with your hands until fully combined, careful not to overwork the meat.

3 Form mixture into 24 balls and place an inch apart on the baking sheet. Bake in the preheated oven for 15-17 mins or until browned and cooked through, careful not to over bake.

4 Remove from oven and serve with tzatziki sauce and greek salad. Store leftovers covered in the refrigerator for up to 4 days. Enjoy!

Calories: 346kcalFat: 29gSaturated fat: 15gCholesterol: 79mgSodium: 507mgPotassium: 415mgCarbohydrates: 4gProtein: 17gVitamin A: 165%Vitamin C: 6%Calcium: 43%Iron: 3.8%

Garlic Bacon Roasted Cauliflower with Herbed Aioli

Serves: 6

Prep Time: 10 mins || Cook Time: 30 min

Cooking Type: Roasting

Course: Main dish

This roasted cauliflower is packed with goodies like crispy savory bacon, garlic, and served with a creamy herbed aioli for dipping.

Ingredients

- 1 head cauliflower cut into florets
- slices nitrate free bacon sugar free for Whole30
- cloves garlic minced
- tsp rosemary fresh, minced
- Sea salt and pepper to taste

aioli:

- 1/2 cup homemade mayo*
- cloves garlic minced
- 1/2 tsp fresh lemon juice
- 1 tsp minced fresh herbs I used sage, rosemary and thyme
- Sea salt and black pepper to taste

Instructions

1 Preheat your oven to 425 degrees. Spread cauliflower florets in a single layer on a large baking sheet. Cut bacon into pieces, then sprinkle all over cauliflower.
2 Roast in the preheated oven for 15 mins, then stir and return to single layer. Continue to roast another 5 mins or until bacon is mostly crisp, then, sprinkle with the garlic and rosemary.
3 Continue to roast another 5-7 mins or until all is toasty. Once done, sprinkle with sea salt and pepper to taste (remember the bacon adds salt, so be careful!)
4 During the last 5-7 mins of roasting, whisk together all aioli ingredients in a small bowl. Serve alongside the cauliflower for dipping. Enjoy!

*You can also use a paleo store bought Mayo version, but I highly recommend starting with my easy homemade recipe for the best flavor.

Calories: 230kcalFat: 22gSaturated fat: 5gCholesterol: 22mgSodium: 270mgPotassium: 112mgCarbohydrates: 2gProtein: 3gVitamin A: 25%Vitamin C: 10.2%Calcium: 16%Iron: 0.4%

Mexican Cauliflower Fried Rice

Serves: 6

Prep Time: 15 mins || Cook Time: 15 mins

Cooking Type: Stove Top

Course: Main dish

This Mexican Cauliflower Rice is packed with veggies, protein, and lots of flavor and spice! It's topped with an easy guacamole and chipotle ranch sauce for a tasty, filling meal that's Paleo, Whole30 compliant and keto friendly.

Ingredients

- 12 oz riced cauliflower about 1 head, just shy of 4 cups
- 1 lb ground beef turkey, chicken, or pork
- 3 Tbsp cooking fat coconut oil, bacon fat, olive oil, ghee, divided
- 1/2 tsp fine grain sea salt
- 1/2 tsp onion powder
- 1/2 tsp garlic powder
- 1 tsp cumin
- 1 tsp chili powder
- generous dash chipotle pepper (adjust to your taste or omit for AIP)
- 1 red bell pepper diced
- 1 small yellow onion diced
- 3 garlic cloves minced
- 1 can chopped green chilis
- 1 jalapeno pepper seeds removed and minced
- Cilantro for garnish
- 1/2 cup homemade chipotle ranch dip
- 1 batch easy guac see below:

easy guac:

- 1 large ripe avocado or 2 small, mashed
- 2-3 Tbsp onion minced
- 1 clove garlic minced
- 1-2 Tbsp jalapeno peppers minced
- 1 1/2 Tbsp fresh lime juice
- 2 Tbsp chopped fresh cilantro plus more for garnish

Instructions

1. Prepare the chipotle ranch, cover and chill until ready to serve.
2. Heat a skillet over medium heat and add 1 Tbsp coconut oil.
3. Add ground meat to skillet and sprinkle with salt and spices. Once browned, add onion, pepper and stir, cook about 45 seconds until softened.

4   Add chopped green chilis, garlic, and jalapeno pepper and continue to cook another 45 seconds to heat through. Add cauli rice and stir to coat, then cover skillet for 30 seconds to soften cauliflower, remove from heat.
5   Before serving, mash together all the guac ingredients in a bowl. To serve fried rice, top with extra cilantro, chipotle ranch and guac. Enjoy!

Calories: 335kcalFat: 27gSaturated fat: 12gCholesterol: 53mgSodium: 273mgPotassium: 604mgCarbohydrates: 9gFiber: 4gSugar: 2gProtein: 15gVitamin A: 855%Vitamin C: 63.8%Calcium: 36%Iron: 2.3%

Crispy Paleo Chicken with Creamy Mushroom Sauce

Serves: 5

Prep Time: 10 mins || Cook Time: 35 min5

Cooking Type: Baking

Course: Main dish

This crispy paleo chicken with creamy mushroom sauce is made all in one skillet, packed with flavor, dairy free, paleo, keto and Whole30 compliant! Seasoned crispy skinned chicken thighs with a dairy free mushroom sauce that's perfect over cauliflower rice or with roasted and veggies

Ingredients

- 5-6 bone-in skin-on chicken thighs
- Sea salt and and pepper to season chicken
- 1 tsp dried sage
- 1/2 tsp dried thyme
- 3 Tbsp olive oil divided
- 8 oz white mushrooms washed and sliced
- 1/2 medium onion chopped (or 1 small)
- 2 cloves garlic minced

- 8 oz chicken bone broth
- Sea salt and pepper
- 1/4 cup full fat coconut milk blended prior to adding
- 2 tsp spicy brown mustard
- 2 tsp tapioca or arrowroot starch

Instructions

1. Preheat your oven to 400 degrees
2. Heat a large cast iron skillet (or any oven proof skillet) over med-high heat. Season chicken with salt, pepper, sage, and thyme, rubbing in seasonings to coat skin.
3. Add 2 Tbsp olive oil to skillet, then brown chicken in skillet on both sides - about 2-3 minutes per side.
4. Once browned, remove chicken from skillet to a plate and lower heat to medium, add 1 more tbsp ghee to melt.
5. Add onions and cook one minute until softened, then add mushrooms and garlic and continue to cook 3 minutes over med heat until softened. Season with salt and pepper to taste, stir in broth, and remove from heat.
6. Return chicken and any juices back to skillet, place skillet in preheated oven and bake 25 minutes, until cooked through, return skillet to stovetop.
7. Remove just the chicken from skillet with tongs to make the sauce. Whisk tapioca and mustard into coconut milk, then add to skillet and whisk to combine. Bring to a boil and allow to boil 2-3 minutes until thickened, stirring. Return chicken to skillet and serve with mushroom sauce. Enjoy! Serves 5-6.

Calories: 437kcalFat: 35gSaturated fat: 14gCholesterol: 164mgSodium: 127mgPotassium: 481mgCarbohydrates: 4gSugar: 1gProtein: 25gVitamin A: 115%Vitamin C: 2.1%Calcium: 18%Iron: 1.7%

Creamy Cilantro Lime Coleslaw

Prep Time: 10 Mins // Cook Time: 35 Mins

Yield: 4

Serving Size: 1/4 of Recipe

Recipe Type: Main dish

A tangy and slightly spicy twist on the classic BBQ side dish.

Ingredients

- 1 14 oz bag coleslaw mix
- 1/2 cup mayo
- 1 tbsp coconut aminos
- 1 tbsp apple cider vinegar
- 1/4 cup chopped fresh cilantro
- 1/2 jalapeno diced
- 1 tbsp fresh squeezed lime juice
- 1/2 tsp sea salt

Instructions

1. Toss all ingredients together in a large bowl and mix well.
2. Best served after chilling in the fridge for at least one hour (and you can also make this the night before!) - Enjoy!

Easy Paleo Broccoli Soup

Serves: 4

Prep Time: 5 mins || **Cook Time:** 10 min

Cooking Type: Baking

 Course: Main dish

This quick recipe is deceptively simple, but it makes a rich creamy soup with a hint of garlic.

Ingredients

- 1 16-ounce bag plain frozen broccoli
- cloves garlic peeled
- cups chicken stock or vegetable stock
- 1 tablespoon ghee or olive oil
- sea salt to taste
- organic extra virgin olive oil for garnish, optional

Instructions

4   Bring broccoli, garlic, and stock to a boil over medium-high heat. Cover, reduce heat and simmer 10 minutes.

5   Carefully transfer to Vitamix and puree until smooth (or puree with an immersion blender).

6   Add olive oil, season with salt, and blend to combine.

Calories: 99kcal | Carbohydrates: 6g | Protein: 4g | Fat: 5g | Saturated Fat: 2g | Cholesterol: 15mg | Sodium: 257mg | Potassium: 189mg | Sugar: 2g | Vitamin C: 1.1mg | Calcium: 8mg | Iron: 0.4mg

Easy Cauliflower Celeriac Soup with Bacon

Serves: 4

Prep Time: 5 mins || Cook Time: 20 min

Cooking Type: Simmering

Course: Main dish

A decadent creamy soup made with cauliflower and celery root.

Ingredients

- 1 16- ounce bag frozen cauliflower
- 1 cup peeled and chopped celeriac
- 2 cloves garlic peeled
- 3-1/2 cups chicken stock or vegetable stock
- 2 tablespoons olive oil
- sea salt to taste
- 4 slices cooked and crumbled bacon
- fresh chives for garnish

Instructions

5   Bring cauliflower, celeriac, garlic and chicken stock to a boil over medium-high heat. Cover, reduce heat and simmer until vegetables are tender, 15-20 minutes.
6   Carefully transfer to Vitamix and puree until smooth.
7   Add olive oil, salt and blend to combine.
8   Top with bacon and chives.

Calories: 238kcal | Carbohydrates: 13g | Protein: 8g | Fat: 17g | Saturated Fat: 7g | Cholesterol: 36mg | Sodium: 349mg | Potassium: 615mg | Fiber: 3g | Sugar: 4g | Vitamin C: 61.6mg | Calcium: 49mg | Iron: 1.1mg

Instant Pot Chicken Broccoli & Rice Casserole

Prep Time: 5 Mins // Cook Time: 15 Mins

Yield: 4

Recipe Type: Main dish

A dairy free, quick and easy version of the favorite comfort food casserole you grew up loving! I've included a low carb caulirice version, as well as a regular rice version!

Ingredients

- 1 lb chicken breasts
- 1 16 oz package frozen cauliflower rice I prefer the texture of frozen vs fresh. I get mine from Costco or Trader Joe's.
- 12 oz broccoli florets
- 1 cup chicken broth
- 2 tbsp olive oil divided
- 1 tsp sea salt
- 1 tsp garlic powder
- 1 tsp onion powder

Instructions

- Preheat your oven to 415. Line a rimmed baking sheet with parchment paper or foil.

- Spread the broccoli florets (and mushrooms if using) out evenly on the pan and drizzle/toss with 1 tbsp olive oil. Sprinkle with salt.
- While the oven comes to temperature, make the caulirice. Select the "sauté" function on your Instant Pot. Add remaining 1 tbsp olive oil and let it heat for a minute or two.
- Add the frozen cauliflower rice with a pinch of salt, and sauté for 5-7 minutes until cooked through. Hit "cancel". Remove the caulirice, place it in a bowl and set aside.
- At this point, you can put the broccoli in the oven. Set a timer for 12 minutes.
- Add the chicken breasts to the bottom of the Instant Pot. Add the sea salt, garlic powder, onion powder, and paprika.
- Pour the chicken broth over top of the chicken and seasonings. Lock the lid, turn the vent to "sealing", and select "manual" high pressure for 10 minutes.
- When the chicken is done, manually release the pressure. Shred the chicken with 2 forks. There will be some extra liquid, but that is a good thing! You don't want your "casserole" to be too dry.
- Add in the cooked caulirice, cooked broccoli, and stir to combine. Select the "sauté" function again. Add the cream cheese and stir well while everything heats together for 2-3 minutes. Hit "cancel". Add salt to taste, serve, and enjoy!

Instant Pot Cider Pulled Pork

Prep Time: 5 Mins // Cook Time: 55 Mins

Yield: 6

Recipe Type: Main dish

Ingredients

- 3-4 lbs pork loin, chops, or shoulder cut into 4 pieces
- 1 medium onion sliced
- 3 cloves garlic minced
- 2 tsp dijon mustard
- 1/4 cup apple cider vinegar
- 1/4 cup chicken broth
- 1/2 cup apple juice or apple cider look for no sugar added
- 1 tsp sea salt

Instructions

1. Place onions in the bottom of the Instant Pot (or slow cooker). Place pork on top of the onions. Whisk remaining ingredients together and pour over the pork.
2. Set your Instant Pot to "manual" 55 mins on high pressure. Let it slow release for about 10-15 minutes, then release the steam. (If using a slow cooker, set on low for 7-8 hours.)
3. Shred the pork using 2 forks. If there is too much juice, hit the "sauté" button and let it simmer until some cooks off. Enjoy!

Roasted Asparagus Avocado Soup

Serves: 4

Prep Time: 10 mins || Cook Time: 10 min

Avocado replaces the cream and makes the soup luxuriously silky.

Ingredients

- 12 ounces asparagus
- 1 tablespoon garlic infused olive oil
- 2 cups chicken stock or vegetable stock
- 1 avocado peeled and cubed
- 1/2 lemon juiced
- 1 tablespoon coconut oil
- sea salt to taste

Instructions

5   Preheat oven to 425 degrees. Or preheat the air fryer to 390 degrees.
6   Toss asparagus with garlic infused olive oil, salt and roast for 10 minutes.
7   Carefully transfer asparagus to Vitamix or high-speed blender with remaining ingredients and puree until smooth. Add salt to taste.
8   Add water to thin to desired consistency, if needed, and warm gently over medium heat. Serve immediately.

Calories: 208kcal | Carbohydrates: 13g | Protein: 6g | Fat: 16g | Saturated Fat: 4g | Cholesterol: 13mg | Sodium: 177mg | Potassium: 560mg | Fiber: 5g | Sugar: 4g | Vitamin A: 715IU | Vitamin C: 17.2mg | Calcium: 34mg | Iron: 2.4mg

Fish and Leek Saute Recipe

Prep Time: 10 minutes || Cook Time: 10 minutes

Yield: 2 servings

Ingredients

- 2 fish fillets (approx. 8 oz or 230 g), diced
- 1 leek, chopped
- 1 teaspoon grated ginger
- 1 Tablespoon (15 ml) gluten-free tamari soy sauce (use coconut aminos for AIP)
- Salt to taste
- 1 Tablespoon (15 ml) avocado oil

Instructions

1. Add the avocado oil into a skillet and sauté the chopped leek.
2. When the leeks soften, add in the diced fish, grated ginger, tamari sauce or coconut aminos, and salt to taste.
3. Saute until the fish isn't translucent anymore and is cooked.
4. Serve immediately.

Chicken breasts stuffed with Mushroom and Spinach and creamed with Coconut Sauce homemade!

Prep Time: 15 Mins // Cook Time: 35 Mins

Servings: 6

Recipe Type: Main

Ingredients:

Preheat oven to 350F

- Chicken breasts (Organic, Grass Fed, Hormone and Anti-Biotic Free)
- 2 Tins Mushrooms (Organic)
- 2 Spinach (In the plastic containers times Two)
- Two Packs of Tarragon
- A Few Stems Rosemary
- 2-3 Cans of Coconut Cream
- 1 1/2 Tsp. Black Pepper
- 1-2 Tsp. Pink Himalayan Salt
- 1-2 Cups Chicken Broth (Organic)
- 4 Head Limes
- 5-8 Cloves Garlic
- 1-2 Head Red Onion

Instructions:

1. Make sure you wash your chicken at all times before you start to cook with.
2. Gently Slice the Chicken Breasts, Flatten them down like "Connected wings" you're going to use a heavy "kitchen Hammer" hammer down (Not too thin).
3. Season the Chicken with Salt and pepper and your desires spice.
4. Grease the chicken with Avocado oil.
5. Chop up the spinach and mushrooms (Finely or your desired size). - Add seasoning on them.
6. Stuff the chicken with the mushrooms and spinach.
7. Have your pan or Iron Skillet ready with the chopped onions and Garlic - Add a bit of Avocado oil to the pan to prevent sticking and of course taste.
8. Add the chicken with the herbs to the pan on Medium high heat - every two minutes you are going to turn the chicken, then you are going to add 1-2 Cups of the Chicken broth, as you do this you are going to put the temperature on Medium heat. Let that simmer for about 5 minutes.
9. Add your coconut cream with the herbs, Lime (Add more salt if needed) for a few minutes 5-7 minutes let that simmer, then you are going to transfer this to the pre heated oven for about 20-30 minutes!.

10. You can enjoy this delicious meal with a big side of Salad and a nice Pesto Dip!

Please Enjoy!

DESSERT

Keto + AIP Friendly Raspberry Coconut Drops

Total time: 1 hr 5 mins

Cook Time:1 hr || Prep Time: 5 mins

Serves:20

Load up on healthy fats with these keto and AIP Raspberry Coconut Drops made with zero refined sugar.

Ingredients

- 1/2 cup coconut butter
- 1/2 cup coconut oil
- 4 T raspberries
- 1/2 t alcohol-free pure vanilla extract

Instructions

1   Place fresh raspberries on parchment-lined baking dish and set in freezer for one hour or until frozen.
2   Meanwhile, stir coconut butter, coconut oil and vanilla extract in a small pot on medium heat. Stir occasionally to help all ingredients fully melt.
3   Remove the raspberries from the freezer and place in a blender. Pulse several times until a crumbly mixture forms.

4   Add the raspberries to the pot with the coconut butter and stir to incorporate well.
5   Spoon the mixture into the silicone molds. Use a knife to flatten and smooth.
6   Place in the freezer one hour or until the coconut drops are solidified.
7   Remove from the freezer and pop the drops out of the molds to serve.
8   Keep in the refrigerator for up to 10 days or in the freezer for 30 days.

FOR AIP: Use alcohol free vanilla or vanilla powder

NOTE: coconut butter is the same as coconut manna or coconut concentrate (should be pure coconut without additives)

Keto Ocean Blueberry Freezer Bites

Total time: 1 hr 5 mins

Inactive Time: 1 hr

Prep Time: 5 mins

Serves: 21

Looking for a tropical treat to cool off with? Try these keto-friendly Ocean Blueberry Freezer Bites made with lemon juice, blueberries, and a hint of coconut.

Ingredients

- 1 cup coconut butter
- 1/2 cup coconut oil
- ½ cup blueberries
- 1 T lemon juice
- 1 t stevia
- 1 T shredded coconut, unsweetened

Instructions

1   Place the coconut butter, coconut oil, blueberries, lemon juice and stevia in a high-speed blender. Blend on high until smooth. You may need to scrape down the sides after blending to ensure the entire batch is smooth.

2   Spoon the mixture into the cavities of the silicone molds. Use a knife to smooth out the tops of each cavity.
3   Sprinkle the shredded coconut over each cavity.
4   Place in the freezer for one hour to set, or until the bites harden.
5   Remove from the freezer and pop the bites out of the molds.
6   Keep in the refrigerator up to 10 days or in the freezer for 30 days.

FOR AIP: use honey or maple syrup to taste, not stevia.

NOTE: If you need to get your coconut butter to a more liquid state I recommend using a double boiler to melt your coconut butter rather than a microwave.

Coconut Butter is the same as Coconut Mana (this is coconut flesh with the oil) - there are recipes in the group for making coconut butter but it can be a little tricky as it's very thick

Chocolate Coconut Truffles

Recipe type: Dessert , Treats

Prep time: 20 mins ||Cook time: 5 mins

Total time: 25 mins

Serves: 4-5

 Decadent coconut truffles with a chocolate coating! Dairy free and nut free!

Ingredients

For the coconut balls:

- ¼ cup water
- 1 tbsp grass-fed gelatin
- 2 tbsp water
- 2 tbsp maple syrup (use maple syrup for AIP and stevia or xylitol for keto version)
- ¼ tsp sea salt
- ½ tsp vanilla extract
- ½ cup coconut flour
- ¼ cup shredded coconut]
- melted coconut oil for greasing palms

For the chocolate coating:

- ¼ cup raw cacao (or carob) [use carob for AIP]
- 3 tbsp melted coconut oil or palm shortening (if using carob, use palm shortening)
- ⅛ tsp sea salt
- 2 drops of vanilla extract
- 1 tbsp raw honey (use raw honey for AIP and xylitol or stevia for keto)

Instructions

For the coconut balls:

1   In a small bowl, add the ¼ cup water and sprinkle the gelatin on top slowly till all of the gelatin is covered with water. Use a fork to spread if required. Keep aside.
2   In a small sauce pan, add the measured quantity of water and maple syrup.
3   Add the salt. As the water begins to boil, turn heat to low and add the wet gelatin mixture to the sauce pan and stir till all of the gelatin is completely dissolved. Add the vanilla extract and stir.
4   Turn heat off. Take the sauce pan from the stove and add the coconut flour and the shredded coconut and mix quickly to form a wet doughy mixture. Let cool for about 2-3 mins.

5   Grease your palms using some coconut oil and then divide the dough into about 8/10 portions and make rounded balls from each portion by rolling between your palms. Keep the balls on a plate.

Making the chocolate coating:

1   In a small mixing bowl, add the cacao powder (or carob).
2   Melt the coconut oil (or palm shortening) before measuring. Then pour the measured quantity into the bowl with the cacao (or carob). Add the salt, vanilla and the honey. Stir quickly to form a smooth chocolate mixture.
3   Immediately dip the coconut balls into this mixture using a spoon and place the coated balls on a tray lined with parchment paper.
4   Place the tray in the refrigerator for about 1 hour to set the truffles before serving.
5   Store the truffles in the refrigerator.

FOR AIP: use quality vanilla (alcohol-free is not required but look for a pure organic

Sugar Cookies

Prep Time: 5 Minutes||Cook Time: 15 Minutes

12 Cookies

Not only are these sugar cookies grain free, nut free, egg free, and paleo but they can also be considered an AIP Keto cookie!

Ingredients

Dry Ingredients

- 1/4 cup tigernut flour
- 1/4 cup coconut flour
- 1/4 cup coconut sugar OR Lakanto sugar – Use coconut sugar if you're following AIP as Lakanto sugar is not AIP elimination stage friendly!*
- 3 tbsp gelatin

Wet Ingredients

- 1/4 cup coconut oil, melted
- 2 tbsp coconut milk
- 1 tsp vanilla

Instructions

1. Preheat oven to 350F.
2. Line a baking pan with parchment paper and set aside.
3. In a large mixing bowl, whisk together all dry ingredients.
4. Then add coconut oil, vanilla, and coconut milk and mix to combine, consistency should be like wet sand.
5. Scoop by tbsp, you may need to give it a little squeeze and form the cookie in your hand to get them to stick together. Then place on the parchment lined baking pan.
6. Bake in the middle of the preheated oven for 15 minuted or until edges are slightly browned.
7. Allow to cool completely otherwise they will fall apart, Enjoy!

Notes

- Lakanto sugar, although Keto, is not considered strict AIP. However, coconut sugar is AIP compliant!
- Store at room temperature or in the refrigerator. Most of my AIP cookies I prefer cold and stored in the fridge.
- However, these ones I prefer to leave them out at room temperature. They are good either way though!

Paleo Snack Mix

Prep Time: 1 hr 15 mins

Ingredients

- 1/4 cup + 2 Tbsp coconut oil
- 4 cups plantain chips
- 4 cups coconut chips
- 1 cup dried cherries or craisins optional
- 1 tbsp garlic powder
- 1/2 tbsp onion powder
- 3 tbsp coconut aminos
- 1/4 tsp himalayan sea salt

Instructions

1. Preheat your oven to 250 degrees
2. Combine plantains, cherries, and coconut flakes in a bowl and stir
3. Melt coconut oil in a large dutch oven on low heat or in microwave and add in garlic powder, onion powder, coconut aminos and sea salt, whisk to combine
4. Add 1/2 of the snack mixture to the liquid and stir to combine
5. Add the second half of the snack mixture and stir well until everything is evenly coated
6. Spread the mixture in a roasting pan or cookie sheet and place it in the oven for one hour, stirring every fifteen minutes

7   Set snack mix aside to cool for 10-15 minutes

Notes

Stores well in an air tight container for 10-14 days!

FOR AIP: ensure your dried fruit does not contain added sugar or non-compliant preservatives

TIP: This makes a big batch, so if you're not sure about it, cut the recipe in half.

Lemon Rosemary Shortbread

Serves: 12-15 cookies

Total time: 30 minutes

Ingredients:

- 1/2 cup coconut flour
- 2 tablespoons arrowroot flour
- 1/2 cup coconut oil or Ghee, melted
- 1 tablespoon lemon juice
- zest of one lemon
- 2 tablespoons maple syrup, raw honey, or liquid sweetener of choice
- 1-2 teaspoons chopped rosemary, fresh is best
- 2 tablespoons filtered water
- pinch of sea salt

optional: 1/4 teaspoon organic lemon extract

Instructions:

1) Preheat the oven to 350F and line a baking sheet with unbleached parchment paper.
2) In a large bowl, mix all of your dry ingredients- coconut flour, arrowroot, salt together.

3) Add melted coconut oil, lemon juice, zest, sweetener, and rosemary. Stir until smooth. If necessary, add the tablespoons of water 1T at a time until a dough forms.
4) Take one tablespoon of the dough, roll into a ball, place on the baking sheet and carefully flatten it. Repeat until the remaining dough has been used.
5) Bake in the oven for 15 minutes.
6) Remove, and cool completely before serving.

FOR AIP: use coconut oil not ghee, use maple syrup or honey as your sweetener of choice.

AIP Lemon Coconut Balls

Makes 12 Balls

Ingredients:

- 1/2 cup coconut flour
- 1/2 unsweetened shredded coconut
- 1/4 cup coconut oil (melted)
- k4 tablespoons raw honey
- 1/2 teaspoon vanilla extract
- zest and juice of one organic lemon

Optional: organic lemon extract for a stronger flavor

Instructions

1 In a mixing bowl, mix all ingredients until combined.
2 Mold the mixture into small balls and refrigerate for 15-20 minutes.
3 Remove when hard

FOR AIP: use quality vanilla (alcohol-free is not required according to the updated AIP

Coconut Ladoos || Coconut Snow Balls

Prep time: 5 mins || Cook time: 5 mins

Total time: 10 mins

Serves: 8-9

Delicious coconut snow balls that are a perfect snack - sweet enough to satisfy your sugar cravings and filled with good nutrients to make it healthy and guilt-free!

Ingredients

- ¼ cup water
- 1 tbsp grass fed gelatin
- 2 tbsp coconut milk

- 2 tbsp maple syrup or honey (use xylitol or stevia for Keto)
- ¼ tsp sea salt
- ½ cup coconut flour
- ½ cup shredded coconut
- ¼ tsp alcohol free vanilla extract or rose extract or crushed dried rose petals
- extra shredded coconut for rolling

Instructions

1. In a small bowl, add the water and then sprinkle the gelatin on top of the water slowly until all the gelatin is wet. Use a fork to further mix and wet the gelatin. Keep aside.
2. In a small sauce pan, add the coconut milk and maple syrup and heat on very low flame. Then add the bloomed gelatin mixture to this and stir continuously while on low heat until all the gelatin gets completely dissolved in the mixture. Now add the salt and turn heat off.
3. To the above mixture, add the coconut flour, shredded coconut and vanilla. Mix using a spoon and then using your hands, form small balls (8-10).
4. Roll each ball in shredded coconut and place on a plate. Place the balls in the refrigerator for about 1 hour to set.

FOR AIP: use additive free coconut milk (water and coconut only), use maple syrup or honey NOT the other sweeteners mentioned - they are NOT AIP, use quality vanilla (alcohol-free is not required)

Veggie Keto Burgers

Prep Time: 15 Mins // Cook Time: 35 Mins

Servings: 6

These are so delicious and super easy to do! I make a huge batch and I freeze them individually in zip lock bags. If you want one or two because they are that GOOD and TASTY you can either toast **them or bake in oven.**

Ingredients:

Optional: Spaghetti Squash or Sweet potatoes 1 Cup - Optional

- 4 Tbl Psyllium Husk Powder
- 1 Cup Chopped Parsley
- 1 Cup Chopped Cilantro
- 1 Cup chopped Kale
- 2 Cups Green Pea
- 2 Large Yellow or White Onions
- 3 Cups Zucchini
- 1 Cup Sun Dried Tomatoes
- 1/2 Cup Mushrooms
- 1 Cup Peppers
- 10 Cloves Garlic
- 3 Whole Lemons
- 2 Tbl Pink Salt
- 1 Tbl Black pepper
- 2 Tbl Paprika
- 3 Tbl Oregano
- 1 Tbl Dried Dill
- 1 Tbl Mustard
- 1/2 Cup Grape seed Oil or Olive Oil

Instructions:

1. Stir Fry everything together.
2. Add more or less spice as you like.
3. Blend everything together except for the Green Pea.
4. Mix everything well.
5. Form into Shapes
6. Bake on 375F for 12-15 minutes
7. Let cool them pack and store in Freezer.
8. Enjoy!

Low Carb Blueberry Muffins

Prep Time: 10 Mins // Cook Time: 30 Mins

Yield: 12

Serving Size: 1 Muffin

Ingredients

- 1/2 cup coconut flour
- 6 tablespoons psyllium husk
- 1 teaspoon baking powder
- 1/2 teaspoon salt
- 1/2 cup unsweetened sunflower seed butter
- 1/4 cup softened coconut oil, ghee or tallow
- 4 large eggs, room temperature
- 3 tablespoons yacon syrup or 1/3 cup honest syrup
- 1/2 cup non-dairy milk of choice
- 1 teaspoon vanilla extract
- 2 tsp. lemon zest
- 1 cup blueberries

Instructions

1. Preheat oven to 350F. Line a muffin tin with cupcake liners.
2. In a large bowl whisk together the coconut flour, psyllium husk, baking powder and salt.
3. In a separate bowl beat together the sunflower seed butter, coconut oil, eggs, syrup, vanilla and milk until well combined and creamy.
4. Add the wet mix to the dry mix and beat until a dough forms.
5. Add in the blueberries and lemon zest and use a spatula to fold in.
6. Use a ¼ cup scoop per muffin. Bake in the center rack for 25- 30 minutes or until the muffins have risen, round and golden on top.
7. Coconut Flour Blueberry Muffins (paleo, keto, dairy free, nut free)
8. Remove from the oven and let cool. Store in an airtight container at room temperature for up to 5 days.

Recipe Notes:

You can also use Zero Syrup which is vegetable glycerin (a sugar alcohol) and monk fruit or Honest Syrup made of vegetable fiber and monk fruit. While the latter is free of sugar alcohols which is ideal for some, it is high very high in total carbs (fiber). Use 1/4 to 1/3 cup in this recipe instead of Yacon Syrup.

Calories: 176.2, Fat: 12.7g, Carbohydrates: 10.4g, Fiber: 6.5g, Protein: 5.2g

Keto Cilantro-Lime Salmon Recipe

Prep: 10 min || Cook: 20 min

Cooking Type: Oven

Serves: 2

Ingredients

- 2 salmon fillets
- 1/2 cup coconut oil, melted
- Juice and zest of 2 limes, and then slice the limes
- 2 garlic cloves, minced
- 1/4 cup fresh cilantro, roughly chopped + more for garnish
- Sea salt and freshly ground black pepper

Instructions

1. Preheat oven to 375 F.
2. Place the lime slices in baking a dish, then season the salmon fillets to taste with sea salt and freshly ground black pepper on both sides; place fish on top of the lime slices.
3. In a bowl, combine lime juice, lime zest, cilantro, garlic, and coconut oil.
4. Pour the mixture over the salmon and place in the oven.
5. Cook 15 to 20 minutes, or until salmon reaches desired doneness.
6. Let the salmon rest 2 to 3 minutes, and serve topped with fresh cilantro and fresh lime slices.

Protein: 50g / 21%, Carbs: 8g / 3%, Fat: 82g / 76%

Lemony Prosciutto-Wrapped Asparagus

Prep Time: 10 Mins // Cook Time: 15 Mins

Yield: 4

Recipe Type: Dessert

A quick and easy side dish or appetizer that is Whole30, paleo, and Keto friendly!

Ingredients

- 16 pieces asparagus ends trimmed
- 8 pieces prosciutto
- 1 lemon
- olive oil or avocado oil spray

Instructions

1. Preheat oven to 450. Line a baking sheet with foil or parchment paper.
2. Cut all of the prosciutto pieces in half. Wrap one half around each piece of asparagus, tucking the ends underneath to hold in place.
3. Place the wrapped asparagus pieces on the baking sheet, making sure to leave some room in between each piece.
4. Spray the pieces of asparagus with oil (lightly). Cut your lemon in half, and squeeze one half over all of the asparagus.
5. Slice the other half into rounds and place them on top of the asparagus. Bake for 12 mins. Enjoy!

One-Bowl Keto Blueberry Muffins

Serves: 12 muffins

Prep Time: 10 mins || Cook Time: 20 min

Cooking Type: Baking

Course: Dessert

These keto blueberry muffins have a crisp top and a soft, fluffy inside! They have a sweet nutty flavor thanks to almond butter and almond flour, and are loaded with plenty of juicy sweet blueberries. They're paleo, gluten-free, dairy-free, and low carb.

Ingredients

- 3 eggs room temp
- 1/2 cup smooth almond butter (a drippier one is best for this recipe)
- 2 Tbsp dairy-free milk almond or coconut
- 1/2 cup erythritol
- 2 tsp pure vanilla extract
- 1 Tbsp lemon juice
- 1 1/4 cups blanched almond flour
- 3/4 tsp baking soda
- 1/4 tsp sea salt
- 1 cup blueberries divided

Instructions

1. Preheat your oven to 325 and line a 12 cup muffin pan with parchment liners.
2. In a large mixing bowl, whisk together the eggs, almond butter, milk, erythritol, vanilla, and lemon juice.
3. Add in the almond flour, baking soda, and salt and mix well with a spatula or spoon, don't over-mix.
4. Fold in 2/3 of the blueberries, then spoon batter into muffin liners to make 12 muffins. Add remaining blueberries to the top of the batter.
5. Bake in the preheated oven for 18-20 minutes or until tops are browning and a toothpick inserted near the center of one comes out clean. Allow to cool in pan for 5 minutes, then transfer to wire racks to cool completely.
6. Once cooled, serve or store loosely covered at room temperature for up to two days, or refrigerate or freeze to keep longer.

Calories: 156kcalFat: 12gSaturated fat: 1gCholesterol: 40mgSodium: 144mgPotassium: 106mgCarbohydrates: 6gFiber: 2gSugar: 2gProtein: 6gVitamin A: 75%Vitamin C: 1.9%Calcium: 70%Iron: 1%

APPETIZER

Roasted Cauliflower Hummus

Serves: 6

Prep Time: 15 mins || **Cook Time:** 30 min

Cooking Type: Roasting

Course: Appetizer

This cauliflower hummus recipe is a perfect blend of tahini, lemon, and garlic.

Ingredients

- 1 head cauliflower cut into florets
- 1/3 cup extra virgin olive oil divided
- 1/3 cup tahini
- 1 clove garlic peeled
- juice of 2 lemons
- 1/2 - 1 teaspoon sea salt to taste

Instructions

1. Preheat oven to 425 degrees.
2. Toss cauliflower florets with 1 tablespoon olive oil and a pinch of salt. Roast on a rimmed baking sheet until fork tender and caramelized, about 20 minutes. Cool completely.
3. Add roasted cauliflower, tahini, garlic, lemon juice, salt, and olive oil to food processor. Process until mixture reaches hummus consistency. Taste and adjust seasonings. Add water, if needed, to thin.

Calories: 211kcal | Carbohydrates: 8g | Protein: 4g | Fat: 19g | Saturated Fat: 2g | Cholesterol: 0mg | Sodium: 33mg | Potassium: 358mg | Fiber: 2g | Sugar: 2g | Vitamin A: 10IU | Vitamin C: 50.7mg | Calcium: 40mg | Iron: 1.1mg

Grilled Eggplant and Roasted Red Pepper Dip

Serves: 6

Prep Time: 10 mins || Cook Time: 45 min

Cooking Type: Baking

Course: Appetizer

Serving size: 1 ½ cups

Grilled eggplant, roasted red pepper, and grill-roasted garlic star in this Italian inspired dip.

Ingredients

- 1 large eggplant
- 1 head garlic
- 1/2 cup diced roasted red peppers
- tablespoons olive oil plus more for drizzling
- tablespoons lemon juice
- 1 tablespoon chopped fresh basil plus more for garnish
- sea salt and fresh ground pepper to taste

Instructions

1. Preheat grill to 400 degrees.
2. Slice top off of garlic, drizzle with olive oil, and sprinkle with sea salt. Wrap in foil and place on grill over indirect heat. Roast until garlic is soft and caramelized, 30 - 45 minutes.
3. Place eggplant on grill and roast with lid closed, turning occasionally, until eggplant is soft, 30 - 45 minutes.
4. Cut eggplant in half and place in colander to drain and cool. Set garlic aside to cool.
5. Peel and dice eggplant. Mash 4 cloves of roasted garlic. Combine eggplant, mashed garlic, peppers, 3 tablespoons olive oil, lemon juice, basil, salt, and pepper. Taste and adjust seasonings.
6. Garnish with an extra drizzle of olive and fresh basil.

Calories: 91kcal | Carbohydrates: 6g | Protein: 1g | Fat: 7g | Saturated Fat: 1g | Cholesterol: 0mg | Sodium: 162mg | Potassium: 210mg | Fiber: 2g | Sugar: 2g | Vitamin A: 95IU | Vitamin C: 10.5mg | Calcium: 20mg | Iron: 0.4mg

Deviled Eggs with Bacon and Chives

Serves: 6

Prep Time: 15 mins || Cook Time: 15 mins

Cooking Type: Baking

Course: Appetizer

Deviled eggs are a quick snack or easy appetizer. This simple recipe is a perfect base for bacon, chives, roasted red peppers, and olives.

Ingredients

- 6 hard-boiled eggs
- 1 tablespoon whole grain Dijon mustard
- 1 tablespoon olive oil
- 1 teaspoon garlic infused olive oil
- 1 - 2 teaspoons lemon juice
- sea salt & pepper to taste

Toppings

- 2 tablespoons crumbled cooked bacon
- 2 tablespoons snipped chives
- 2 tablespoons sliced olives
- 2 tablespoons chopped roasted red peppers

Instructions

1. Peel eggs and slice in half lengthwise. Place egg whites on serving tray and add egg yolks to mixing bowl.
2. Add mustard, olive oils, lemon juice, salt and pepper to egg yolks. Mash with fork until creamy. If needed, add water to thin, one teaspoon at a time. Taste and adjust seasonings.
3. Fill egg whites with yolk mixture and top generously with desired toppings.

Calories: 131kcal | Carbohydrates: 1g | Protein: 7g | Fat: 10g | Saturated Fat: 2g | Cholesterol: 189mg | Sodium: 232mg | Potassium: 79mg | Fiber: 0g | Sugar: 0g | Vitamin A: 340IU | Vitamin C: 3.4mg | Calcium: 27mg | Iron: 0.7mg

Roasted Garlic Baba Ganoush

Prep Time: 10 mins || Cook Time: 45 min

Serves: 8

Cooking Type: Baking

Course: Appetizers

An easy dip recipe that is gluten-free and paleo-friendly made with the traditional ingredients.

Ingredients

- 1 head garlic
- 2 medium eggplant
- 3- 4 tablespoons lemon juice juice of 1-1/2 to 2 lemons
- 2 tablespoons tahini
- 2 tablespoons extra virgin olive oil plus more for drizzling
- ½ teaspoon sea salt

Instructions

1. Preheat oven to 400 degrees.
2. Cut the top off the head of garlic. Place on a sheet of foil and drizzle with olive oil. Wrap tightly in foil and place on a rimmed baking sheet with the eggplants.
3. Roast the vegetables for about 45 minutes, until the eggplants are collapsed and the garlic is completely soft.
4. Cut the eggplants in half lengthwise and place in a colander to cool and drain. Open the garlic packet to cool.
5. Peel the eggplants and squeeze the flesh from the garlic head. Place all ingredients in the food processor and pulse to desired consistency. Taste and adjust seasonings.

Calories: 88kcal | Carbohydrates: 9g | Protein: 2g | Fat: 5g | Saturated Fat: 0g | Cholesterol: 0mg | Sodium: 149mg | Potassium: 300mg | Fiber: 3g | Sugar: 4g | Vitamin A: 25IU | Vitamin C: 6.3mg | Calcium: 22mg | Iron: 0.5mg

Cilantro Lime Dressing

Prep Time: 5 Minutes

Servings Serving Size: 2 Tablespoons

Yield: 8

Five minute, thick and creamy Avocado Cilantro Lime Dressing - fresh, zesty and packs a punch! Use for topping off salads and dipping veggies.

Ingredients

- 1 bunch fresh cilantro | about 2 cups packed - stems and all*
- 2 large cloves |1 heaping tablespoon garlic
- 3 tablespoons | 45 ml lime juice
- 6 tablespoons | 90 ml extra virgin olive oil
- 1/2 teaspoon salt
- 1/2 teaspoon red chili flakes
- 1 avocado
- 1-2 tablespoons water (optional)

Instructions

1   Add all of the ingredients to a blender and blend until smooth. Taste and season with more salt and lime juice as you see fit.

NOTES

- Make sure to wash and dry your cilantro well before using.
- Keep store in the fridge for up to a week

Amount Per Serving: Calories: 122 Total Fat: 13g Saturated Fat: 2g Sodium: 149mg Carbohydrates: 2g Fiber: 1g Sugar: 0g Protein: 0g

FOR AIP: Use honey or maple syrup as your sweetener of choice

Avocado and Lime Agua Fresca

Ingredients

- 1 large ripe avocado
- 1/2 cup fresh lime juice
- 1/3 cup granulated Swerve (or) monk fruit
- 4 cups cold water
- Ice for serving

Instructions

1 In a blender, blend together the first 4 ingredients until smooth.
2 Pour over ice and serve.

Feel free to start with 1/4 cup of sweetener and adjust the sweetness according to your own personal preference.

For AIP: Use honey in place of the sugar alcohol

Made in the USA
Middletown, DE
24 February 2020